7

Argentina: An Economic Chronicle
How one of the richest countries in the world lost its wealth

Argentina: An Economic Chronicle
How one of the richest countries in the world lost its wealth

By

Vito Tanzi

Jorge Pinto Books Inc.
New York

Argentina: An Economic Chronicle
How one of the richest countries in the world lost its wealth

Copyright © 2007 by Vito Tanzi

Published by Jorge Pinto Books Inc., website: www.pintobooks.com

Cover design © 2007 by Susan Hildebrand

Cover Image: Pablo Helguera, "Facing the Unknowable" collage, 2007 from the series *Panamerican Suite*. Courtesy of the artist, website: www.panamericanismo.org

Edited by Noël Baca Castex

Book design by Charles King, website: www.ckmm.com

ISBN 0-9795576-0-7
978-0-9795576-0-6

Contents

Preface

Over the past century Argentina has often attracted the attention of the world. Its size (five times bigger than France and nine times bigger than Italy), its physical beauty (Iguazú, Bariloche, Patagonia), its culture, and, until the earlier part of the twentieth century, its wealth, made it a strong magnet for European emigrants looking for a better life. It is difficult to believe today that, at some point during the last century, Argentina accounted for 7 percent of the world's exports and for half of the gross domestic product of Latin America. In other words, it was a major economic power. For many poor Europeans, the American dream could be achieved in Argentina and not just in the United States. Thus, they moved there in the millions, especially before World War I and after World War II.

The flow of European emigrants toward Argentina continued until around 1950, when Perón was president and in the process of creating a welfare state. At that time, Argentina was still a rich and welcoming country where poor immigrants from Europe were not discriminated against and where they could live comfortably, eat well, and hope that their children would move up socially. The welfare state Perón created, possibly the first one in the world, along with Uruguay's, contributed to the attraction that Argentina held for those who left Europe. Then, European immigrants stopped coming. A couple of decades later, some even started going back to the places they had come from. Argentina started the twentieth century as one of the world's richest countries and ended it with a lot of poverty and the stigma of having experienced the largest default on foreign debt in the history of the world.

Economists are very interested in—and often talk and write a great deal about—economic development. This is the process, observed in many countries, by which poor nations become rich. Strangely, there is no good word to describe the reverse experience—the process by which a rich country becomes poor. If such a word existed (impoverishment comes close), it would describe what happened to Argentina over the past century, especially during the second half of it. There are now several good books written by economists and economic historians that, with the help of numerous statistics, describe the process of the progressive impoverishment of Argentina. The aim of this book is not to provide another technical description

1

of its economic decline. Rather, it is mainly to provide a description of the changes that took place over half a century, through episodes I participated in as an employee of international institutions and, especially, as a senior staff member of the International Monetary Fund. Over the course of more than three decades, I visited Argentina at least thirty times and have spent, cumulatively, several months there. This privileged position put me in contact with many of those making economic decisions as well as with economists and regular citizens. As a result, I was able to observe policy in the making, to occasionally participate in that process, and to witness the effects of the policy decisions as well. This opportunity is rarely experienced by writers of economic books.

This book has not been written for specialists, but for the general reader with some interest in Argentina and a minimum background in economics and fiscal issues. Readers who found Joe Stiglitz' book on globalization (*Globalization and Its Discontents*) interesting should also enjoy this book. I have used a simple style with minimal economic jargon in order to keep the freshness of a "memoir" and to make it accessible to a wide range of readers. Those with an interest in economics and fiscal matters should find the descriptions of fiscal developments of particular interest. But the book covers more than just economics so those without a background in economics should still be able to enjoy it.

The book contains several stories that will help make particular points and that, I hope, will entertain as well as inform the reader. These stories should provide an intuitive appreciation of what happened to this fascinating country over the past half century. Considering the events that occurred in recent years, I could not fail to address the relationship between the country and the IMF. This relationship has been much in the news and has been strongly criticized in recent books such as Joe Stiglitz' *Globalization and Its Discontents*, Paul Blustein's *And the Money Kept Rolling In (and Out)*, and Ernesto Tennembaum's *Enemigos*. My book discusses this relationship in a couple of chapters and finds much to criticize in the role of the IMF. However, the reasons I present are different from those given by the authors mentioned above.

Modern books are expected to fit within distinct categories. The modern world likes to classify things. Thus, there are books that deal with economics, travel, cultural developments, politics, cooking, and so on. This book does not easily fit in any specific category because, being largely a memoir, it describes events, places, and people as they were seen by the author during his many trips. Some of these descriptions will be enjoyed by those who are interested in Argentina, but less by those who are interested in economics only. There are two specific filters that have affected the narrative: The first one is the author's professional background; the second one is his national background. Being an economist and an Italian from the south of Italy, the area from which many of the poor immigrants came to Argentina, have inevitably colored the description.

Numerous people have contributed, directly or indirectly, to the writing of this book. Many of them have been mentioned in the various chapters. I have resisted the temptation, common among writers, of providing a long list of names. The objective of these long lists seems to be mainly impressing the reader. However, there are a few people who could not be ignored.

I am especially grateful to four Argentine friends who have carefully read earlier drafts of the manuscript, given me advice and corrected mistakes. My great thanks go to Alieto Guadagni, Humberto Petrei, Mario Teijeiro and especially Carlos Silvani. They are all well known and knowledgeable Argentine economists who have held important positions during various Argentine administrations and/or in the Argentine financial system. Because I did not always follow their advice, they are not responsible for any remaining errors or for any opinions expressed. For these I am strictly and solely responsible. I am also grateful to Domingo Cavallo, Eduardo Cavallo, George Kopits, and Axel Radics, who have read later versions of the manuscript and have also given me valuable suggestions. Again, they are not responsible either for any errors or particular interpretations of events.

In an informal and non-technical way, I have used a particular and novel theory to explain the macroeconomic economic developments of Argentina during the past half century. This theory has justified the original title of the book, for, during that period in Argentina, it was "mostly fiscal." The theory concerns the existence of "fiscal cycles." In other words, fiscal developments were the driving force in generating macroeconomic disequilibria. The verification of this theory—though informal and impressionistic—required the use of good fiscal statistics spanning five decades. Damian Bonari, director of Analysis of Public Spending and Social Programs of Argentina's Ministry of Economy, was kind enough to provide me with official historical data that has allowed me to verify the theory. I am most grateful to him.

Closer to home, I must thank the InterAmerican Development Bank (IDB), which provided a convenient place during much of the time I was writing the book. During that period I was working as a consultant for that institution. Needless to say, the IDB is in no way responsible for the views herein expressed. Jesusa Hilario patiently and competently typed various drafts; to her goes my deep appreciation. Finally, I must thank my wife, María, for the many times we stayed home instead of going out because I wanted to work on the book, and for the "space" that she's provided me for writing, mostly on weekends. At times, she's had to live with a "zombie" who was totally absorbed in his work and showed no interest in contributing to the house chores.

Vito Tanzi
July 2007

CHAPTER I

Perón and the Creation of

the Permanent Fiscal Problem

With the exception of Italy, where I was born and have spent the first twenty years of my life and a few additional brief periods, and the United States, where I have spent much of my professional adult life, there is no other country I have been more involved with—and have visited more often—than Argentina. Over the past four decades, I have visited that country at least thirty times and have spent more than a full year there considering my many visits. During these years, I have seen it evolve from a country whose per capita income was close to Italy's (and half that of the United States) to a country whose per capita income fell to about a third of Italy's and a fifth of the United States'. This change has undoubtedly had an impact not only on the economic, but also on the psychological conditions of the Argentine people. Argentina has had the same experience of a family who was rich and became poor. It is not easy to adjust to the new position. This may explain why Argentina has one of the highest ratios of psychologists per person in the world.

The last four decades have seen dramatic political and economic developments. The country went from military governments to an elected (Peronist) government in 1973; back to military governments from 1976 to 1983; then finally, back again to democratically elected governments. Politically, the changes have been in the right direction. Unfortunately, the same cannot be said on the economic front. With the exception of the first half of the 1990s, when Argentina had the fastest growth rate in Latin America, these four decades were not good. In 2004, Argentina's per capita income was not much higher than forty years earlier and, in 2001, Argentina declared the largest debt default in the history of the world. The long term consequences of that default are hard to predict.

The above-mentioned developments are puzzling because Argentina does not seem like a place where they could occur. The country has both natural resources and human capital, conditions that should lead to a prosperous economy. Its schools are fairly good and its population well educated by Latin American standards and, a century ago, even by European standards. Argentina's cultural life has been and continues to be very rich. For example, its Colón Theater, built at the beginning of the twentieth century, is still one of the greatest opera houses in the world. In the first part of the last century, that theater was visited regularly by the most famous opera singers and music directors at the time. Argentina has produced architects, scientists, musical conductors, composers, writers and other cultural and scientific personalities who have become world-famous. Five of its citizens have won Nobel Prizes—three of these in medicine or chemistry (in 1947, 1970, and 1984). Several Argentine economists hold or have held positions at top American universities. Furthermore, besides the fact that the country is far from major world markets, it is a large nation blessed by good climate, some of the most productive land in the world (the Pampas), a long coast line, and an abundance of mineral resources including petroleum. The ratio of natural resources to the population is high. It also has extraordinarily beautiful sites that make it an attractive destination for tourists. In short, a Martian visiting Earth for the first time would guess that it is one of the world's richest and most successful countries. In fact, if the Martian had landed on Earth a century ago, his guess would have been right. Unfortunately, this is a case in which, at least for the past half century, the whole has been much less than its parts. Somehow, Argentina has been like a newborn with good genes who, after an initial growth spurt, failed to grow to his potential.

My objective in this book is not providing an organized description of the developments that occurred in Argentina but, rather, to share the impressions gathered from my visits and to describe particular experiences. I hope that these impressions will help convey a feel for the country and the developments that have taken place there. For these descriptions I have relied almost exclusively on my recollection of events and the information collected during these trips. I have refrained from making this a book based on research. As a consequence, there are no footnotes and very few references to published sources.

I visited Argentina for the first time in 1969. At that time, I was teaching at the American University in Washington, D.C. and working as a consultant for the Joint Tax Program, a program within the Organization of American States. This program was financed jointly by the OAS, the InterAmerican Development Bank (IDB), and the United Nations. In 1969, the Joint Tax Program opened a training center in Buenos Aires called Centro Interamericano de Estudios Tributarios (CIET; InterAmerican Center of Tributary Studies). The purpose of this center was to give courses on taxation geared toward employees of the tax administrations of Latin American countries. At that time, low tax ratios were considered a major obstacle to economic growth because they constrained the presumably positive role that governments could play in the development of their countries.

The Director of the Joint Tax Program in 1969 was a distinguished-looking lawyer from Buenos Aires named Manuel Rapoport. He was a tall, sophisticated and cultured gentleman married to an equally attractive and elegant lady. This couple was typical of the sophistication that prevailed in Argentina at that time. For about a century, Argentina had been a prosperous country with a great sense of culture. As a recent article put it: "By 1910 . . . Argentina was one of the foremost countries in the world. It was one of the most important grain and meat exporters. Its GDP represented 50 percent of all Hispanic America, ranked 10th in the world's economy, and its trade amounted to 7 percent of the world's total." (See José Ignacio García Hamilton, 2005. "Historical Reflections on the Splendor and Decline of Argentina". *Cato Journal*, vol. 25, no. 3; 528.) In 1913, its per capita income was higher than that of France, twice that of Italy, and almost five times that of Japan. (See Maizels, Alfred. *Industrial Growth and World Trade.* Cambridge [Eng.]: Cambridge University Press, 1963.)

Argentina was a magnet for European immigrants and its citizens felt particularly close to the European culture because most of their ancestors had come from Europe. Argentina considered itself a largely European country that, due to an accident of geography, had ended up in the south of Latin America. At that time, it had no inferiority complex vis á vis other countries. A joke illustrates this attitude: When an Argentine visited Rome and was trying to locate in the phone book someone he had to meet, he was surprised by the large number of Argentine last names he saw in the Italian phone book! In a visit to my house in Washington, D.C., Mr. Rapoport was surprised.that I did not have any tango records. This must have seemed a big shortcoming in my cultural background. Tango has characterized Argentina more than any other cultural activity.

Manuel Rapoport decided that I would be the first teacher at the opening of the CIET courses in Buenos Aires. The course would be on tax reform and would be given in Spanish. By this time, I had been working as a consultant for the Joint Tax Program for five years and had picked up enough Spanish to be able to understand it and be understood when I spoke using a mixture of Italian and Spanish. As an undergraduate student, eight years earlier, and stimulated by the fact that I was dating Olga, a beautiful Cuban young lady, I took a summer course in Spanish, which gave me some basic Spanish skills. Still, my fluency was limited and I felt uncomfortable at the thought of giving hours of lectures in Spanish to Spanish-speaking individuals. Mr. Rapoport did not want to listen to my arguments and decided that I should be the one to go to Buenos Aires and give the first course at the opening of the CIET.

In the 1960s, Buenos Aires was still one of the largest, richest, and most beautiful cities in the world. Its per capita income was well above that of the rest of Argentina. I still recall my amazement at the size of the city as the plane prepared for landing. The city seemed to never end. I had decided to go to Buenos Aires a few days before the beginning of the course in order to prepare for it and to visit the city I had heard so much about. I found the place spectacular. I was particularly impressed by the large parks, the wide avenues, the quality of such buildings as the Ministry of Foreign Affairs, and the immense shopping areas that seemed to never end. I recall being really impressed by the sight of dog walkers, young men who, for a fee, would walk the dogs of affluent owners through the city parks. At times, they would have as many as twenty well-behaved dogs on a leash. This was a paid activity that I had never dreamed existed. It could only exist in a wealthy society.

I recall walking along the famed Calle Florida, with its many shopping arcades; Harrods; and the traditional coffee shops, places for cultural meetings and social gatherings. Graham Greene wrote about one of these coffee shops, Confitería Richmond, in his book, *The Honorary Consul*. This was where the elegant ladies of Buenos Aires went to eat profiteroles and spend their afternoons gossiping and discussing their romances and love life. I remember the beautiful shops of Avenida Santa Fe, the movie houses and restaurants of Calle Lavalle, and the cemetery of La Recoleta, a graveyard in the middle of one of the most elegant quarters of Buenos Aires. At that time, La Recoleta claimed to have the most expensive land per square foot in the world. Thus, one had to be very rich to be buried there. There were parts of Buenos Aires that reminded me of Paris and that, in fact, had been built as a challenge to Paris. The *porteños* (the vernacular for the inhabitants of the city of Buenos Aires) referred to these areas as "rincones de París" (corners of Paris). Buenos Aires even had its challenge to the Champs Elysées, with the Avenida 9 de Julio, which claimed to be wider than the famous Parisian boulevard, and to the Paris Metro, with the city's own elegant subway system built in 1911. The Linea A of the Buenos Aires subway, which goes from Plaza de Mayo to Plaza Miserere, was one of the finest in the world. The artwork in its stations competed with that of the Paris Metro. As a sign in the InterAmerican Development Bank describing an exhibition on the Buenos Aires of the 1880–1920 period put it: "The Buenos Aires of a century ago sought openly and without inhibition to emulate the great urban centers of Europe, not only in matters of physical appearance but also in intellectual and social life. During that period, the city [of Buenos Aires] occupied a privileged position in the Americas."

In the late 1960s, Buenos Aires still looked much more interesting to a visitor than Washington, D.C., especially at that time when, due to high crime rates and riots, D.C. was a dull and, especially at the center, a largely empty city. On weekends and in the evenings, D.C. looked like a ghost city where a neutron bomb had been dropped. The buildings were there but there were no people. On the other hand, Buenos Aires seemed to be a much larger and richer version of southern Italian cities where life seemed to never stop. It was crowded, noisy, full of life; it had the colors, and even the smells, of Italian cities. One could walk at two o'clock at night and find the streets teeming with people. The scent of freshly roasted coffee and grilled steaks was everywhere. I marveled at the size and the taste of the "bife de chorizo," the famous Argentine steak. I also had the strange feeling of being at home despite the size of the city.

At that time, the per capita income of Argentina was about the same as Italy's. Italy had been undergoing what was called the "Italian miracle," a period of fast economic growth, while the growth rate of Argentina had slowed down. However, in spite of the fast growth rate of Italy, the per capita income of Buenos Aires in the 1960s was still much higher than that of the Mezzogiorno (the south) of Italy, where I was born and where my parents still lived. I had no doubts that the many Italians who had emigrated to Argentina after World War II (some even from the town where I was born), had made a good choice. They had become totally integrated in the new country. I thought they were lucky compared to those who had stayed behind in Italy or, perhaps, even compared to those who had gone to the cold, impersonal, industrial cities of the United States. I understood why those who had emigrated to Argentina had not gone back to Italy—unlike many who had emigrated to the United States and returned to Italy after accumulating some assets. Culturally and even climatically, Argentina—or better, Buenos Aires—was much closer to Italy than the United States was. People went to the United States to earn money and to Argentina to create a new life. Paraphrasing the title of an Italian book by Laura Pariani, *Quando Dio Ballava il Tango* (When God Used to Dance the Tango; Rizzoli, 2002), this was a time when God was Argentine.

During the few days before the course started, I contacted the brother of Florian Bade, a German friend of mine, who was working as an economist at the OAS in Washington. Florian insisted that I contact his brother who had migrated from Germany to Buenos Aires some years earlier. I called the gentleman and was invited to visit his house for the weekend. I had to take a train and a bus because he lived outside of Buenos Aires, which was no problem because, at that time, Buenos Aires was a safe city and public transportation was good. When I got there, in the afternoon, I was introduced to his wife and told that some other people would be coming over for dinner that night. Mr. Bade invited me to join him on a flight over Buenos Aires in the small two-seater plane he owned, which was parked at a nearby airport. Thus, I had the opportunity to see Buenos Aires through the privileged perspective of a small plane that could fly at low altitude over many important sites. Mr. Bade pointed out to me many landmarks. I remember that it was a clear and beautiful day. I enjoyed the flight even though I had never been on a small plane before. Back at the house, his wife informed me that this was the first time her husband had flown the plane after he broke a leg a few months earlier in a landing that had not gone too well! I do not know whether I would have accepted the invitation to fly if I had received this information before the flight; or whether I would have enjoyed it as much.

In spite of my limited Spanish, the course went relatively well. I compensated for my rudimentary language skills with my knowledge of the subject matter. At that time, most economists believed that developing countries badly needed more tax revenue to promote growth through the financing of public investment. Public investment was regarded as the engine of growth. Interestingly, today there are some economists and many political leaders who are convinced that there is a huge "infrastructure gap" in Latin America, and that more investments in infrastructure would produce growth. However, reflecting the changes in time, they would prefer to finance these investments through loans and not through taxes, accepting a "golden rule" that argues that investment spending should be netted out when measuring the size of fiscal deficits. The United Kingdom has made this position popular among some groups. My lectures focused on a country's "taxable capacity," explaining why higher tax revenue would be beneficial to a country and, especially, how to get more revenue. At that time, the view was that particular variables, such as per capita income, urbanization, share of agriculture in the economy, and mineral exports determined a country's potential to raise tax revenue; that is how its "tax capacity" was determined. A country was expected to make an effort to move closer to this potential. As it would often happen in those years, in this and in similar courses, I met individuals who would later assume important positions in their governments.

In 1969, Argentina was run by a military government under the leadership of General Onganía. The economy minister of the province of Buenos Aires, the most important of the Argentine provinces, was Dr. José Maria Dagnino-Pastore, an economist who had studied at Harvard in the early 1960s, when I was a student there. Dr. Dagnino-Pastore found out that I was in Buenos Aires and, on the last day of the course, invited me to dinner at his official residence in La Plata, a town not far from Buenos Aires, where the provincial government was located. He sent a car to pick me up. I was happy to see him and his charming wife, and very much enjoyed the elaborate dinner that had been prepared. Over dinner, I learned about the economy of Argentina and about the fiscal arrangements between the national government and the powerful provincial governments. I learned that provincial governments and, especially that of the province of Buenos Aires, were politically very important. Dr. Dagnino-Pastore would become economy minister for brief periods in 1970 and 1982.

On the way back to the hotel, located near the Casa Rosada, the presidential office, I developed a bad stomach ache. By the time I got to the hotel, Hotel Nogaró, I was very sick. I recalled that, on that day, I'd had lunch at an Italian restaurant and ordered fish soup. Obviously, the fish was not fresh and I had a case of food poisoning. In all my years of travel all over the world, this was the worst case of food poisoning I ever had. The fact that this had occurred in Buenos Aires was embarrassing to my Argentine friends. I spent the next two days in bed at the hotel eating raw apples, boiled rice, and drinking large amounts of tea to prevent dehydration. Hugo Gonzales-Cano, whom I had met at the CIET, who would become a good friend over many years, helped me contact a doctor and get some medication. He was married to Marina, a pleasant lady of Italian background and they both spoke Italian well, as many Argentines did at that time. This medical problem spoiled part of my first trip to Buenos Aires because it cut short the social part of it.

Between 1969 and 1972, I went back to Buenos Aires a couple more times for short visits, but I do not have specific impressions from these visits. In 1973, I was engaged as a consultant in World Bank missions to Haiti and Ecuador, and in a tax conference in Mexico organized by the OAS. I spent much of 1974 in Italy, on a sabbatical year, with a grant from the Bank of Italy. As a result, I did not visit Argentina during the turbulent Peronist years between 1973 and early 1976. On my return from Italy to Washington, in August of 1974 I took leave from my academic position at the American University and joined the IMF as head of the Tax Policy Division in the Fiscal Affairs Department. In 1981, I was promoted to director of the Fiscal Affairs Department, a position I would hold until my retirement from the Fund at the end of 2000. During those years, the Fiscal Affairs Department had probably the biggest concentration of Ph.D.'s with a background in public finance in the world. The department followed the fiscal developments in the Fund's member countries. Through my new affiliation with the IMF, I would be involved with Argentina at different times and for different purposes starting in 1976.

The military government of General Onganía was followed by other military governments headed by General Levingston (1970–1971) and General Lanusse (1971–1973). Lanusse took the first step toward democracy, by allowing the reestablishment of political parties, and made a commitment to return Argentina to democracy. In March of 1973, elections were held and the Peronist party won. In October of that year, a second election was held and Juan Domingo Perón was elected president of Argentina and his wife, María Estela Martínez de Perón, called Isabel, became vice president. Perón and his wife had been living in Spain until then. Perón died in July of 1974 and was succeeded in the presidency by his wife. Isabel was his third wife; they had married in Spain in 1961.

Perón had been vice president of Argentina from 1944–1946, and president of Argentina from 1946–1955, when a military coup forced him out and into exile in Paraguay, Panama and Spain. In those years, he transformed Argentina. It is difficult to understand future developments in the country without knowing what happened during that period. In that transformation, Perón was assisted by his wildly popular and charismatic wife at the time, Evita Perón. Evita was so popular, especially among the poorer classes of Argentina, the "descamisados," those without shirts, that when she died of cancer on July 26, 1952, her remains were embalmed and many called for her sainthood. By 1950, she was probably the most powerful woman in the world. As a biographer put it: "[Evita] was the emotional center of Peronism and provided it with a heart and a soul." (See Joseph Page's introduction to Evita's presumed autobiography, *In My Own World, Evita;* The Free Press, 1996; 18). She was the ultimate populist and a model for future populists.

Perón had been influenced both by the corporatist fascist policies of Italy, where he was the Argentine military attaché during Mussolini's regime, and by the socialist policies of Russia. He and Evita created a political movement that tried to merge these two contrasting ideologies. Thus, Peronism appealed to both leftist and rightist groups. In time, this would create tensions within the movement between the right-wing and the left-wing strands of Peronism, as each tried to establish its supremacy. In the nine years he was president, between 1946 and 1955, he used the enormous rents that the country was then receiving from its exports of agricultural products—at a time (during and after World War II) when these products were very much in demand—to establish a welfare state with universal benefits for workers and their families and for the creation of powerful, but government-controlled, unions in every industry. Evita played an important role in linking Peronism to the unions. The Argentine welfare state (together with that of Uruguay) might have been the first one to be established in the world. At that time, it was well ahead of the European ones in terms of the share of public spending into GDP and in terms of social legislation.

Between 1940–1944 and 1945–1954, the share of public spending into Gross Domestic Product rose by about 10 percent of GDP, to around 30 percent of GDP. This was an extremely high level for the time, probably higher than in any other country in the world. To this, one should add the social spending of the gigantic Eva Perón Foundation, which was financed by extra-budgetary, but not spontaneous, "contributions" from workers and enterprises. This increase in public spending was used to finance pensions, education, training, public housing projects, vacations, and guaranteed free medical care for workers, extended paid leave for pregnant workers, and many other social programs.

To facilitate the extraction of high rents from commodity exports, Perón established an export monopoly: the Argentine Institute for Promotion of Exchange. In this respect, he followed the practices of socialist countries. The institute bought commodities from domestic producers at much lower prices than the the commodities would be sold abroad. This left the government with high revenues, which were implicit export taxes. It was one way of transferring income from the agricultural to the urban, industrial sector. Perón also depleted pension funds originally planned under the capitalization or actuarial approach to pensions. He nationalized many foreign-owned enterprises, including the railroad and the tramway system, which he bought from its British owners. He paid for the latter with assets accumulated during the war and temporarily frozen in British banks. In the process, he ran large fiscal deficits, especially in the earlier years. However, the nationalization of public enterprises gave him access to many jobs that he could use for political purposes.

The link between Peronism and the trade unions created an institutional network that, in future years, allowed the Peronist movement to control several activities, including social programs and many jobs. Peronism would remain a powerful political movement with mass appeal, especially in the cities, for decades to come. Its existence would make it difficult for future governments to substantially change the role of the state that was created during the Perón regime. However, the ideological fragmentation or split personality of the movement, particularly in the 1973–1976 period, would create major difficulties because some groups, especially those from the left side of the movement, felt alienated from the current policies pursued by the Peronist government. In their view, Peronism had taken a sharp turn to the right and away from Evita's legacy.

A different and longer-lasting problem was created by the welfare state policies established in the 1946–1955 period. These policies promoted and legislated an economic role of the state, that is an implicit set of promises to the citizens that required large public spending and, therefore, large public revenue to contain fiscal deficits and avoid fiscal difficulties. After World War II, the financing of public spending had been facilitated by the reserves accumulated during the war and by large rents from the export of commodities (although these rents had not been sufficient to finance all the spending). Future governments would not have those rents and would find themselves with a welfare state that the country could no longer afford. When this happens, and countries are unable to politically change the legislated role of the state, they generally try to cut spending administratively or they look for non-permanent and non-ordinary means of financing, including borrowing and the printing of money. This creates situations where public spending tends to continually exceed ordinary public revenue. Fiscal deficits become the norm and the quality of public services deteriorates creating constant pressures for more spending. In these situations, a country is left with an inefficient and under-financed welfare state and with continuous macroeconomic difficulties. This happened to Argentina with a vengeance and characterized the half century after the first government of Perón. It is a lesson that should be learned by countries now undergoing large yearly fiscal deficits such as Italy.

The situation created is what could be called "fiscal cycles." In particular periods, governments with stronger political power and determination managed to temporarily bring public spending and ordinary public revenue close to equilibrium. But this equilibrium was not a stable one. In time, it would be replaced by a large and unsustainable fiscal deficit which would, again, require big fiscal efforts. Fiscal cycles become permanent features in these situations. We will see evidence of these cycles during the decades that followed the first Peronist government.

CHAPTER II

The Military Takeover of 1976 and the IMF Missions

After the death of Perón in July 1974, his wife Isabel became president. Many Peronists who had revered Evita could not stomach Isabel who, in their view, was the usurper of the former first lady's rightful legacy. Isabel lacked the charisma of Evita and the relationship that Evita had with workers and poor people. Also, the fact that Perón had distanced himself from the leftist part of the Peronist movement after his return from Spain, put Isabel in a difficult political situation. She was caught in the middle of the fight between the left and the right wings of the Peronist party. Terrorist movements became active and criticism against Isabel Perón became louder.

Terrorist groups, which had appeared around 1969 and assassinated General Aramburu, became progressively more daring. Major newspapers reported stories about the weakness of Argentine institutions in the fight against terrorist groups such as the Montoneros and Ejército Revolucionario del Pueblo (ERP). Perón had supported these leftist groups as counterweights to the power of the military, but he rejected them later. In March 1973, the Peronists were back in power. The Peronist elected president, Héctor J. Cámpora, had appointed several leftists to his cabinet, which set him against the right-wing tendencies of Peronism. This led Perón to ask for his resignation and new elections in which Perón was elected president by more than a 60 percent majority. By 1975, Argentina was having growing political and economic difficulties. The rate of inflation had risen to 183 percent and the fiscal deficit had reached 14 percent of GDP. The government was loosing control over both the economic and the political situations.

I recall reading a story about a young woman who had belonged to one of these terrorist organizations and had been captured and imprisoned during the military governments. When the Peronists regained power, after 1973, they released presumed "political" prisoners from jail, including this woman. Soon after her release, she wrote an article for a magazine describing in detail, and without any sign of guilt, how she had murdered Pedro Aramburu, who had succeeded Perón as president of Argentina in 1955–1958 and was later kidnapped and executed by terrorists. Terrorists groups had also killed the President of Fiat Argentina, Oberdán Salustro, as well as several union leaders, and had managed to get an extraordinary ransom of $55 million (US dollars) for the release of Jorge Born, an extremely wealthy Argentine magnate. An interesting sideline is that the kidnapping of Mr. Salustro was decided by the kidnappers after one of the secretaries working in the Tax Administration stole a confidential list containing the names of the Argentine citizens with the highest declared incomes. Mr. Salustro's name had been on the list, which was stolen from the desk of Mr. Carlos Silvani, who would later join the IMF and, in the 1990s, become Argentina's director of taxation. Mary Anastasia O'Grady, an American journalist, reported in an article in the *Wall Street Journal* (July 23, 2004; A13) that between May 1973 and March 1976, when the military returned to power, there were 5079 terrorist attacks and 400 murders, including those of 100 civilians. She based her story on a book by Vicente Massot titled *Matar o morir* (to kill or to die).

These terrorist acts caused in many Argentines the desire to return to normalcy. The natural desire for law and order (always present) would be fundamental in the country's easy military takeover in March 1976, as it also was perhaps in the more difficult takeover of Chile by the military on September 11, 1973. In both cases, the concept of "justice" had acquired a nuanced form in the periods before the coups. It was more related to the perception of what was just, on the part of those in the governments, than to the respect of the rule of law. Radical or revolutionary movements have often experienced difficulties with existing laws, which they see as unfair and as protecting the interests of those in power. Thus, they tend to be impatient about the "rule of the law." But breaking existing rules often creates the conditions for counter reactions, because the rules are often broken against the interest of normal and less radicalized citizens.

In the mid-1970s, military governments were in control in Bolivia, Brazil, Chile, Paraguay, Peru, and Uruguay. Therefore, in the face of the ongoing, increasingly chaotic situation, it seemed only a matter of time before the Argentine military, still a major force in Argentine society, would act and return to power. At the time, some American newspapers were surprised at the reluctance shown by the military to seize power. After their earlier experience, the military did not seem overly anxious to return to power. According to an Argentine source, the military had reportedly been told in advance that the current U.S. government would recognize a new military government, thus, removing a major obstacle to their return. See, for example, Mario Rapoport et al's *Historia Económica, Política y Social de la Argentina, 1880–2000* (Buenos Aires: Ediciones Macchi, 2000; 725).

The military coup came on March 24, 1976. That March, the inflation rate had reached 1000 points per year. The coup was led by Generals Jorge Videla (army), Emilio Massera (navy), and Orlando Agosti (air force). A military "junta" took control. By this time, the Argentine economy was undergoing a major crisis with an accelerating inflation rate, disappearing foreign reserves, growing fiscal deficits and unemployment, and a falling output. In 1976, the rate of inflation would rise to 444 percent per year. Between 1970 and 1976, and especially after 1973, when the Peronists had returned to power, the economic situation began to go downhill. The "junta" installed an economic team made up of José Alfredo Martínez de Hoz, Juan Aleman, and Adolfo Diz, all highly competent and serious individuals. Adolfo Diz, who became president of the Central Bank, had a Ph.D. in economics from the University of Chicago. The new team immediately contacted the IMF to negotiate a program of financial assistance.

By late May 1976, an IMF mission was in Buenos Aires to attempt to put together a program that could be taken to the Board of Executive Directors of the Fund. Once approved, financial resources would be made available to the Argentine government. This would allow the government to make many and much-needed policy changes that would, hopefully, bring the economic situation back to normal. The program would require numerous missions to Argentina. I was part of the Fund's negotiating missions and, over the following two years, would visit Buenos Aires several times and spend many weeks there. I was the only member of the IMF missions who did not change in those two years. Thus, I became a kind of reference point for Argentineans.

In the many years I spent at the Fund, these were in certain ways among the most dramatic missions I participated in. The missions were also intellectually stimulating because they encouraged the writing of papers that made significant contributions to economics and to economic policy. Through what came to be called the "Tanzi effect," these papers added to our understanding of how economies function in periods of high inflation. During the inflationary periods of the 1980s and early 1990s, the "Tanzi Effect" became widely cited. It was often referred to by ministers of countries undergoing severe inflation and even by the media. It was also mentioned in several economics textbooks. I will describe that effect later.

In May 1976, an IMF mission led by an American, Jack Gunther, a division chief in the Western Hemisphere Department of the IMF, the department formally responsible for negotiating financial assistance programs, and three other Fund economists, traveled to Buenos Aires to begin the data gathering and the negotiations for the financial program that the Fund would agree with the Argentine government. I recall that during the three weeks that the first IMF mission spent in Buenos Aires, the weather was damp, gloomy, windy, and cold. This was the time of the year when the days in the Southern Hemisphere are the shortest. This fact, combined with the constantly low clouds, made Buenos Aires look like Helsinki must look in December. But what made this and successive Fund missions depressing was the fact that Argentina was in the middle of a civil war between the military and the police on one side, and terrorist groups on the other. This created an atmosphere of fear and constant danger, which restricted our movements and depressed us.

Then, Buenos Aires looked very different from the way it had looked in 1969, when I first visited the city, even though only seven years had passed. I came to appreciate how much the sun and the atmosphere in general contribute to the way we react to places—they can make us love or dislike the same place. The change in the appearance of Buenos Aires was due partly to the weather, partly to the political and security situation, and partly to the economic crisis. Beggars had appeared in the streets, which had not been well maintained, making the city look much poorer and less well kept than I recalled from earlier visits. What Argentines call "villas miseria," urban slums, had spread around Buenos Aires.

Upon arrival at Ezeiza, Buenos Aires' international airport, we were met by representatives of the government and by a large group of individuals carrying weapons, including machine guns. They belonged to the national police and would be our bodyguards for the three weeks we would stay in Buenos Aires. There were twenty-four such guards assigned to protect us from assassination attempts, who would rotate so that eight of them were constantly with us day and night. During the day, they would escort us wherever we went. At night, they would guard the corridor outside the rooms of the Sheraton Hotel, where we were staying. They would also occupy the rooms in the floors immediately below and above our hotel rooms as a precaution against the placing of bombs. This did not seem to be an unnecessary precaution because a bomb had detonated at the Sheraton a few weeks before our arrival.

I recall that one evening, when we returned from our meetings at the Ministry of Economy, next to the Casa Rosada, the door to my room was open, and I found one of the police officers who were escorting us inspecting the room. I asked him what he was doing and he replied that he was checking for bombs. He wanted to be sure that, during the day, nobody, including hotel personnel, had placed a bomb in the room. The impression that we got was that they did not trust *anyone*, even the drivers of our official cars who were regular government employees or hotel personnel. Our bodyguards told us not to reveal our schedules or whereabouts to anyone, including our drivers.

Upon leaving the hotel in the morning, we would be escorted by police cars in front and behind our car. They would use-two way radios and code numbers to inform other police officers about our movements. They would say, for example, that "mobil 3" (unit 3) was headed for "destinación 5" or something similar. The cars would often drive on the wrong side of the street while a policeman, protruding from an open window, would shout and gesture to oncoming cars and trucks to get out of the way. I never understood why they did this. I became convinced that there was a much greater chance of being killed in a car accident than in a terrorist attack.

At that time, the members of the IMF mission had some knowledge of the economic developments in Argentina, but knew little about social or political events. The Fund was supposed to follow closely the economic developments of countries but not the political ones, and to deal with whatever government was in control at the time. The nature of these governments, whether democratic or authoritarian, was considered irrelevant. The economists working at the Fund were not encouraged to get involved in, or even to become knowledgeable about, political issues. At that time, the IMF did not find anything strange about its dealings with the government of Ceaucescu in Romania, or, in later years, Mobutu in the Congo. They both had financial programs with the IMF, as did various dictators from other countries, including Marcos in the Philippines. Then, concerns about corruption, governance, and democratic processes had not yet made their appearance. As long as a government was firmly in power, the Fund was expected to be indifferent to its political nature. It was expected to be politically neutral. For staff members, there was no incentive to learn about political developments, except for those that could have short-run economic implications as, for example, the approval of a budget or a tax reform. Much of what we knew about politics in Argentina we learned from occasional newspaper articles and, especially, from what our police escorts told us. The fact that the same individuals were with us all the time for weeks, and that several of them were of Italian background—some even spoke some Italian—made them be particularly open with me.

They told us that the Montoneros or the ERP, the two main terrorist organizations, were intent on disrupting normal activities and causing chaos. Because of the prominence of the IMF, and the fact that we were in Buenos Aires to help the (military) government, we would be prime targets for terrorism. Thus, extreme precautions were necessary. Some of these bodyguards came from families that had several members in the police or in the military. Some told us that members of their families had been killed by the terrorists. Today, with the access to information available, and with the emotional impact of movies and books that have stressed the oppressive nature of the military regime, there is a tendency to regard the developments of that period as a war by the military against more or less innocent victims, who happened to have leftist ideas. However, to us at that time, and probably to our bodyguards, it seemed more like a civil war in which atrocities were committed on both sides; it was a civil war that had started before the March 1976 military coup. But there is no doubt that, because of the situation we were in, we had a clearly biased view of the ongoing events. We certainly knew nothing about torture, the disappearance of people, and other atrocities. These probably started or intensified in the months that followed the military coup.

The Sheraton Hotel in Buenos Aires faces a large plaza with the famous British tower in the center of it. On the other side of the plaza is the main railroad station, Retiro. The Argentine railroads were built by the British at the end of the nineteenth century. In an act of nationalistic fervor, economic stupidity, and perhaps political opportunism, Perón nationalized the railroad system paying a large amount of money to its British owners. This act of nationalization was surely not a good one because the infrastructure was already in Argentina and there was no need to spend money to buy it. However, the money used was funds frozen by the British government that could not be used by Argentina in the short run. The buying of this and other enterprises allowed the Peronist government to place several of its supporters in the nationalized enterprises. It allowed the government to control one of the "commanding heights" of the economy. Employment in the railroad went up sharply and productivity went sharply down. Many of the workers employed in them did little that was genuinely productive.

When the railroad was privatized in the early 1990s, during the Menem era, employment in it fell dramatically and productivity went up again, but many areas of the country ceased to be serviced by the railroad, leading to growing discontent. Some distant small towns literally died in the process. This raises the obvious question of whether a government has the responsibility to keep alive towns that no longer have an economic "raison d'être." Public enterprises had been inefficient but they had played a significant role in providing services and jobs to poorer people. Many of those employees who had worked for the railroad and who lost their jobs during the Menem administration could not find other jobs. This was mainly due to their limited human capital, but also to the belief from many that these individuals had developed bad working habits. It was considered that they had never worked in the true sense of the word, so they would not be productive in other jobs. And, given their ages, their bad habits could not be changed. During the Menem era, unemployment would go up in spite of the fast growth of the economy, especially in the early 1990s. The creation of public enterprises was one of the instruments that the government had used to establish an inefficient but, to some, a real system of social protection.

The Sheraton Hotel was practically empty during that first mission. I had the impression that we were the only guests at the hotel. The head of the mission, perhaps as an indication of his concern about safety, had all his meals in his room and socialized little. The rest of us would most of the time eat in the hotel's large coffee shop. Venturing out of the hotel meant dragging along several of our bodyguards and we did it only rarely. We were usually the only customers in the hotel's large dining room. After a few days, we noticed that a relatively young man had started to come to the coffee shop at about the same time we did and, despite the fact that the room was rather large and empty, he always sat as close to our table as possible. We became concerned about his presence. Given the worries about terrorism and what were reading or hearing about in the news, we reported the presence of the young man to our police escorts. He did not show up the next day, and we never saw him again. Our questions to the bodyguards were met with vague answers. Considering what I read years later about the "desaparecidos," people who simply vanished, I could not help thinking about the guy and what might have happened to him. I also felt a bit guilty.

Years later, I learned that thousands of Argentines vanished during that period. Current estimates of the large numbers have ranged between 9,000 and 30,000. Presumably, these people were killed by military or paramilitary forces. Some pregnant women disappeared after having delivered babies. In some cases, the babies were adopted by the same individuals who had been instrumental in the women's disappearance. Some of these children would grow up to discover that their "parents" were actually the executioners or members of the group that had ordered the execution of their biological mothers. Some movies, like the Oscar-winning *The Official Story*, have dealt with this sad matter. During what came to be called the "dirty war," the Navy Mechanics School, known as ESMA, became a concentration camp. This school has recently been made into a Museum of Memory.

During one of these missions, we were invited to an "asado," a weekend cookout, by the interior minister, who controlled the security forces and the national police. We were happy to do something different that would break the monotony of fifteen-hour workdays and highly restricted movements—we had been experiencing feelings of claustrophobia. The morning of the "asado," however, we were informed that the invitation had been cancelled without explanation. Later, I learned from Ricardo Arriazu—an economist who had been on the Board of the IMF representing Argentina and who was now an adviser to Adolfo Diz, the Central Bank's president—that the cancellation of the cookout was due to security concerns. Apparently, the government had received reliable information that an attack on the mission was being planned. At this point, I became truly worried. I realized that the situation had to be really bad if the interior minister, who controls the police force, is unable to assure the safety of a small group during a social event in his house.

At the time, there was no highway connecting the center of Buenos Aires with the airport. The road to the airport went through some of the poorest areas of Buenos Aires and got flooded whenever it rained, so cars had to move slowly or even make detours through heavily-populated marginal areas. This created a significant security problem. In fact, at the end of the first mission, there was concern about our transfer from the hotel to the airport. At some point, the possibility of transporting us by helicopter was discussed. However, when the time came to leave, it was decided that a strengthened police escort would accompany us.

We left for the airport in the late afternoon because the flights to Miami and New York depart in the evening. A little convoy followed us. It traveled without problems until it reached the airport, where there was a checkpoint manned by airforce personnel. The convoy was asked to stop. Our escort explained who we were and asked that the convoy be allowed to go through. But the military at the check point refused, explaining that only airforce personnel were allowed to carry weapons into the airport. They asked our bodyguards to leave their weapons behind, but the police refused and an argument ensued. Both sides became so excited that I was afraid they would start shooting at each other. It was definitely a scary moment. A seemingly long time went by before higher ups were contacted and the police was allowed to go through with their weapons. I still recall the sense of freedom we felt when the plane finally took off and we were en route to Miami. We all applauded the take off. We had lived a three-week nightmare.

The mission was back in Buenos Aires in the middle of the Argentine winter, in July or August 1976. The technical work was slow and the government was starting to introduce some of the necessary policies. These policies required a reduction in credit expansion, increases in taxes, cuts in public spending, the elimination of some tax incentives, a better control of the spending of the public enterprises, and other similar policies. By that time, the economy minister, Martínez de Hoz, a very urbane, gentle, and cultured individual who spoke perfect English with a British accent and reminded me of an English don, started to be referred to as Martínez Dios (Martínez "God") or "Hood Robin." The reason was that Robin Hood robbed the rich to help the poor, while Martínez de Hoz robbed the poor to help the rich. In reality, the gentleman was just trying hard to bring some stability to the Argentine economy.

The public enterprises during that period were running large deficits that contributed to a huge fiscal imbalance that was being financed by the printing of money, thus contributing to inflation. There were various reasons for the deficits of the public enterprises. The most important were: (a) the low controlled prices they charged their customers for their services; prices that always lagged behind inflation; (b) the attempt to provide services (such as transportation and electricity) to far away places regardless of costs; (c) the large number of individuals who abusively used the services without even paying the low prices charged; (d) the excessive employment in those enterprises; and, perhaps, (e) corruption connected with the high prices that the enterprises paid to private providers of goods and services. High-ranking militaries were in charge of some of these enterprises and there were questions about the transparency of the enterprises' accounts. In Argentina there was a sort of military industrial complex made up of public enterprises run by the military. Some of these produced weapons.

In a military government, the civilians in charge of economic policy have limited power over high-ranking military officials. What economists call "principal-agents problems" become particularly significant. These problems arise when the agents do not carry out the instructions they receive from their principals. In these situations it becomes difficult at times to determine who is the principal and who is the agent. Thus, we found ourselves in the unusual situation of being urged by the (civilian) economic policymakers to try to get data on the finances of the military enterprises that they were unable to get directly. This was particularly important for the public petroleum company Yacimientos Petrolíferos Fiscales, known as YPF. This company was so huge and so important that it was believed to have a budget almost as large as the national budget. However, its budget was not known. Because petroleum companies do not need to hire too many workers and can export part of their output, it was believed that YPF had a large surplus that could help finance the rest of the government.

The members of the mission decided that it was essential for the IMF program being negotiated with Argentina that we had access to the accounts of YPF. Thus, we started exerting pressure to schedule an appointment with the chairman of YPF. After several calls, we were finally able to arrange a meeting with him. We prepared the questions to ask and went to YPF's headquarters at the agreed time. We were ushered to a large room and asked to wait. We did not mind waiting—we were happy that we would finally get our data. After a while, a distinguished-looking gentleman entered the room and we got up to introduce ourselves to the chairman. Alas, the man was not the chairman but only his secretary. He explained, with a straight face, that the chairman had had to travel unexpectedly out of the country and did not know when he would return. The chairman (a general) sent his apologies. We were invited to leave our questions and were assured that we would soon receive the answers. Obviously, we were annoyed by this turn of events but there was nothing we could do. We left the questions but never got any answers. This episode has helped to convince me that economists often do not appreciate how little control ministers may have on parts of the public sector. It has also convinced me that the Fund should worry more about the introduction of specific policies and less about statistics. At that time, the IMF's Western Hemisphere Department, the department responsible for Argentina, had a true obsession with numbers, which were religiously entered in what was called the "black book."

By late 1976, the security situation seemed to have worsened. This was the time when Operation Condor must have gotten underway. Ironically, this operation was probably one of the first global, or better, international coordinated actions against "terrorism." Of course, at the time nobody had heard of this operation, which had been coordinated by the various military governments of the countries in the Southern Cone to get rid of presumed terrorists and leftists. What, at least in Argentina must have started as a genuine anti-terrorist operation, became an anti-leftist operation that was increasingly directed against people whose main fault was having left-wing ideas. Obviously, we were unaware of this development and continued to be concerned about our safety because terrorist acts continued to happen.

I remember well the night, at the end of the second mission, when we were supposed to return to Washington after spending the usual two–three weeks in Buenos Aires. It must have been July or August 1976. That evening, while we were at the hotel preparing to leave for the airport, a young woman had gone to a military club to meet an officer she was dating. She was carrying a bag, which she left on a chair at the club while, she said, she was going to buy some cigarettes. While she was gone, the package exploded and killed about fifteen high-ranking officers. We received a phone call and were informed that our flight would leave at 4:00 a.m. instead of the usual 11:00 p.m., so we would be picked up before 2:00 a.m. This made it impossible to go to bed. Later in the evening, another phone call announced that we would be picked up not at 2:00 a. m. but at 4:00 a.m. Finally, we reached the airport with the usual heavy escort at about 5:00 a.m. We spent the next twelve hours in the airport because, I presume, for reasons connected with the previous night's terrorist act, the plane would not leave until the afternoon. I recall that the IMF's managing director was supposed to report to the board the next morning on the work of the mission in Argentina and he needed to be fully briefed. Thus, when we got to New York in the middle of the night, we rented a car and drove to Washington to be able to brief the Fund's managing director in time for the opening of the meeting of the board. We had not slept for two nights. This was the joy of life at the Fund sometimes! It was not always five star hotels and expensive restaurants.

Incidentally, perhaps as a reprisal against the bombing, a few weeks later about thirty individuals detained by the police were taken to a place outside Buenos Aires called Fátima and shot. Afterward, their bodies were blown up with dynamite. This came to be referred later as the massacre of Fátima.

CHAPTER III

Inflation, Tax Revenue, and the "Tanzi Effect"

During the several IMF missions to Argentina, in the 1976–1978 period, my main responsibility as the fiscal expert in the missions was to understand what was going on and to assist the Argentine authorities in improving the fiscal situation. In 1975, the year before the first mission, there had been a dramatic deterioration in the already precarious fiscal situation. This deterioration had, to some extent, contributed to the conditions that led to the military coup. In 1975, the fiscal deficit had reached 14 percent of the country's gross domestic product, possibly a record in the history of Argentina. The level of taxation at the central government level had collapsed to only 8 percent of GDP and to 12 percent of GDP for the whole public sector, including the taxes paid to the social security administration and the provincial and municipal governments. These figures do not include the always present off-budget social contributions paid by workers and employers.

The financing of the huge fiscal deficit, mostly through the printing of money, had led to a skyrocketing rate of inflation that reached 183 percent per year in 1975, and 444 percent per year in 1976. Therefore, a highly important and urgent objective was to reduce the fiscal deficit, mainly by raising the level of taxation. The sharp reduction of net transfers to the industrial sector after 1975, a reduction that contributed to a large reduction in public spending in 1976 and 1977, was not enough. These transfers had reached very high levels in 1975, the last full year the Peronists were in power, contributing to the high level of public spending in 1974 and 1975. Thus, much attention would be directed to the tax system. Over the 1976–1978 period, the level of taxation for the public sector would rise from 12 percent of GDP in 1975 to 17 percent of GDP in 1978, while the fiscal deficit would fall from 14 percent of GDP in 1975 to the still high level of 5 percent of GDP in 1978. After 1978, the situation began to deteriorate once again, mainly because of increasing public spending.

As I mentioned when I discussed the Peronist policies introduced in the 1946–1955 period, since Perón's time, Argentina has had a fundamental, dynamic, long-run disequilibrium in its public finances. The problem is that the spending responsibilities of the public sector—the ones reflected in the country's legislation—*under normal circumstances* tend to exceed substantially the normal level of taxation; that is, the level that citizens seem disposed to pay and the tax administration is capable of collecting. Occasionally, the equilibrium in the fiscal accounts is established through *exceptional* tax efforts and through *unsustainable* administrative cuts in public spending. These exceptional tax efforts, just because they are "exceptional," cannot be sustained for long. Sooner or later, those who are behind these efforts grow tired or lose the support of the politicians. When this happens, tax revenue returns to more normal, lower levels. "Unsustainable" cuts in public spending, by definition, cannot be sustained for long. They involve sharp cuts in public investment, and in operation and maintenance spending on the existing infrastructure, leading to a deterioration of the infrastructure; large reductions in real wages for public sector employees; increasing delays in payments to suppliers; the non-replenishment of normal supplies; and so on. This puts the country in the situation of a person who, in order to lose weight, reduces his intake of food well below what his body needs and increases his physical activity beyond the level that his body can sustain. For a while, this regimen can be successful; however, it is unlikely that the new weight will represent a long-run equilibrium.

Only a fundamental, legislated redimentioning of the government's responsibilities in the economy (i.e., in the constitutional or legislated role of the state) to a level of public spending consistent with the normal, sustainable level of taxation, can bring equilibrium in the fiscal accounts. This equilibrium, in the long run, will bring the ordinary revenue of the government in line with its long-run spending level. So far, no Argentine administration has been able or willing to pay the political price for such a reduction in the role of the state. To give a rough sense of quantification to the problem, I would venture the guess that the long-run level of public spending has exceeded the sustainable level of public revenue by, say, about 10 percent of GDP.

In 1975 and 1976, the level of taxation fell below the long-run normal level. Several factors contributed to the sharp fall in tax revenue in those years. Some of these factors were of a permanent character; others were transitory. I will mention some of these factors, but I will focus on one especially, i.e. the effect of changes in the rate of inflation on tax revenue. Let me start with the more permanent factors: A first factor to consider is the quality of the tax system. Argentina has, and has had, many able tax experts. Public finance and taxation is an area with many followers in the country. The Argentine Association of Tax Experts (economists, accountants, lawyers) has more than 40,000 members and Argentine economists monopolize the Latin American participation in the annual meetings of the International Institute of Public Finance. Some of these experts have advised other countries on how to have better tax systems. However, for reasons that are not easy to understand, and that must be associated with sociology and not economics, this expertise has not been translated into a good tax system and tax administration at home. The explanation that one would often hear in Buenos Aires is that Argentines do not like to pay taxes. When I would comment that nobody likes to pay taxes, I would be given a look that implied: "you just do not understand."

With the exception of some transitory periods, the Argentine tax administration has been dysfunctional. In 1975–1976, this degree of dysfunction reached extreme levels. The tax administration suffered from many problems. First of all, it had become a relaxed place where many employees received full-time (though much compressed real) salaries but worked for only few hours a day. Many of these employees, while on the payroll of the tax administration, had private practices where they spent much of their working day advising the same taxpayers they were supposed to be administering on how to reduce their tax liabilities. Some were corrupt and, for a bribe, would take care of the tax problems of some taxpayers. They would use their power in the selection of audits, in the determination of fines, in the (intentional) misplacing of relevant files, in selecting taxpayers for inspections, in estimating the income or sales of taxpayers, and so on. Some, especially those in high positions, would accommodate requests from politicians to go easy on some taxpayers and, perhaps, to be severe with others. As one employee put it, "you interpret the law for friends and clients and apply it rigidly for others."

In Argentina, and in several other Latin American countries, the tax administration did not enjoy the political independence it ought to have. Its power was very limited. In the rare cases when taxpayers who had evaded large amounts of taxes were brought before the judicial system for punishment, those in the judiciary could be bought as well. In fact, Argentina provided evidence that a weak judiciary can make tax administration very difficult. This is an example of what I have occasionally called "institutionally generated negative externalities": A dysfunctional institution affects negatively the functioning of other institutions. In Argentina a dysfunctional judiciary made the work of the tax administration much more difficult.

The inefficiency of the tax administration made it easy for clever taxpayers to develop strategies to minimize their payments. Regarding income taxes, a simple strategy for many was not reporting income, on the realistic assumption that the tax administration was too inefficient to discover taxpayers who did not present a declaration, the so-called "non-filers." This was particularly easy for non-dependent workers such as the self employed and those who had small businesses. Thus, the income tax became largely a tax on high salaries paid by the government or by large and often foreign enterprises. As for the value-added taxes, the strategy was printing false invoices for inputs purchased from suppliers who were (presumably) located in far away provinces; or from those whose address was that of a building that had recently been demolished; or even, from enterprises that had recently disappeared. Some taxpayers would read with attention announcements of bankruptcy in newspapers and print invoices of goods bought from those enterprises.

These and other strategies made it easy for enterprises and small businesses to evade paying taxes or to reduce their tax payments. The larger enterprises could rely on tax avoidance schemes made possible by the complex legislation and by the impact of inflation. For these enterprises, the real cost of taxation was the need to have accountants to deal with taxes. This was a major cost for smaller enterprises. In addition, the existence of tax incentives offered to certain faraway provinces made it possible for some businesses to claim that their activities were located in those provinces. As it was often said, only the invoices may have been produced in the provinces that benefited from the incentives, not the goods.

The tax system itself was very complex, which complicated the tasks of the tax administration and the compliance of the taxpayers. I recall making a big point at the time about there being no less than 96 different taxes collected, even excluding those imposed on the provincial or municipal level. I started a campaign toward simplification of the tax system, pointing out that some of the 96 taxes cost more to administer than they provided in revenue. This campaign produced some results and, in time, the number of taxes was sharply reduced. A paper I wrote at that time helped produce similar results in other Latin American countries.

I also campaigned strongly for the removal of taxes on exports that had survived from Perón's time. A tax on exports is the equivalent of a tax on production combined with an equivalent subsidy to the local consumption of the taxed product. It is clearly a bad tax. These taxes had a long history in Argentina, they were the taxes that had made possible the extraction of high rents from the exports of agricultural commodities, especially during the time of Perón. These inefficient taxes reduced foreign revenues at a time when the country desperately needed foreign reserves. The (incorrect) argument that these taxes were shifted to the foreign buyers was often heard. This shifting could occur only if Argentina had a monopolistic power on the exported products, which was clearly not the case. In time, these taxes disappeared, to reappear, presumably on a temporary base, in recent years. As is well known, temporary taxes, like unwanted guests, have the bad habit of staying around for a long time.

In addition to these more or less permanent factors, there were factors of a more transitory nature. I will briefly mention one and discuss another one at length. In 1976, a major tax problem was caused by the fact that public enterprises that sold particular services to other public enterprises, or to the government itself, were often not being paid for the services or the products sold. This occurred with transportation services, electricity, petroleum and others. Because these enterprises were not being paid (sometimes by the government itself) they started not paying their taxes or the services they bought from other enterprises. By the way, this was also a big problem in the early 1990s in Russia, where at one time so-called tax arrears reached 6 percent of GDP. This created a matrix of arrears that complicated the financial transactions in the whole system and reduced the tax revenue that the government received. In Argentina, it took several years to disentangle the mess created by these arrears.

The other impact on tax revenue, an impact that could be considered of a short-run nature, had to do with the effect inflation, and especially high and accelerating inflation, had on tax revenue. The sharp fall in tax revenue in 1975 and 1976 had led to a great deal of discussion and various hypotheses on its cause. This fall was contrary to the prevailing economic theory, which assumed that inflation, by pushing the income of individuals into brackets taxed at higher marginal tax rates, and by expanding some nominal incomes such as interest received and capital gains, would lead to an increase in the real tax revenue, thus raising the ratio of taxes into GDP.

The prevailing theory then, based on the "fiscal drag" hypothesis, was being empirically challenged in Argentina by the fact that the real tax revenue was going down and not up, as predicted by that theory. Two alternative explanations were offered in the newspapers or discussions for the fall in real tax revenue. One was that, at that time, the tax administration had somehow become less efficient than in earlier years. This may have been true, but it was unlikely to explain the large and rather sudden drop in revenue. It is unlikely that a tax administration could change so much, so rapidly. A second explanation was that, in a period of high inflation, people are faced with an increasing scarcity of money. As a consequence, they increase their normal rate of tax evasion making tax revenue to fall. I found this explanation not convincing either. Somehow, the thought that when there is too much money, money becomes scarce, and that this leads to more tax evasion did not sound plausible. A more sophisticated version of this second hypothesis was that, as inflation rises, banking intermediation shrinks and credit becomes more scarce. Thus, taxpayers begin to delay paying taxes to the government. While this alternative explanation had more credibility, I did not find it entirely convincing either. I felt that there had to be a better theory or explanation for this phenomenon. Incidentally, similar falls in tax revenue had been reported for periods of high inflation in other countries. In his classic study of the German hyperinflation in the early 1920s, Costantino Bresciani-Turroni, an Italian economist, described a similar phenomenon. The same happened in Chile at the end of the Salvador Allende administration.

I began to sense that the explanation must be somewhere else and that it might have something to do with the rate of inflation and with the time that passed between the occurrence of a "taxable event" and the actual payment of taxes to the government in relation to that event. The legal obligation to pay a tax (the tax liability) takes place when certain events occur. For example, the obligation to pay a tax on income takes place when income is earned. The obligation to pay a tax on sales occurs when an item subject to the sales tax is sold. The obligation to pay a tax on imports occurs when goods cross the frontier. All these taxable events establish a claim by the government from taxpayers and an obligation by the taxpayers with the government. However, for practical or administrative reasons, the actual tax payments were not being made immediately at the time the taxable event occurred, but some time later. In some cases, much later. For example, taxes on this year's income may not be due until next year. Taxes due on the sale of goods and services may not be paid to the government, by the seller of the goods who withholds the taxes from the consumers (say a shop), until sometime later, perhaps 30 or 60 days later. These delays in payment (these collection lags), have little importance when there is no inflation or when the rate of inflation is low. However, the higher the rate of inflation becomes, the lower the *real* value of the payment received by the government is compared with the value it would have if it had been made immediately after the taxable event; that is, without any delay. Thus, the collection lag becomes a fundamental variable in the determination of real tax revenue in situations of high inflation. The significance of this lag had not received attention from tax experts and economists.

With the rates of inflation that prevailed in Argentina, and in some other countries such as Brazil, Chile, Bolivia, Mexico, Peru, Russia, etc., in the 1970s, 1980s, and early 1990s, the size of the collection lag became very important. For example, a collection lag of, say, two months, which was normal for the payment of sales taxes such as the value-added tax, combined with a *monthly* rate of inflation of 10 percent, would lead to a reduction in real tax revenue of some 20 percent. A *monthly* inflation rate of 20 percent would lead to a fall in real tax revenue of about 40 percent. At times, these and even higher rates of inflation occurred in several countries in recent decades. In the early 1990s, Brazil's monthly inflation rate was more than 30 percent and, in 1989 Argentina, it would be even higher. It is therefore easy to see why an accelerating inflation that reached a very high level could dramatically reduce the tax revenue of a country even without higher tax evasion or a deteriorating tax administration. Furthermore, the higher the initial level of taxation is, i.e., the higher the share of taxes into GDP at zero inflation is, the larger the *absolute* revenue loss for the country will be. For example, an accelerating rate of inflation that causes revenue to fall by, say, 20 percent from its original level, will imply a loss of 2 percent of GDP if the initial level of taxation (the ratio of taxes to GDP) was 10 percent, and a 6 percent of GDP loss if the initial tax level was 30 percent of GDP.

In conclusion, the higher the rate of inflation is, the bigger the average collection lag for the whole tax system is; and the higher the initial (at zero inflation) share of taxes into GDP is, the greater the negative impact of inflation on a country's tax revenue will be. Given these three variables, the impact of inflation on tax revenue can be estimated. It should be understood that, ceteris paribus, an accelerating rate of inflation *reduces* tax revenue while a decelerating rate of inflation *increases* tax revenue. This last insight became important when for example, in 1991, Argentina introduced the so-called "convertibility plan" that tied the peso to the dollar, abruptly reducing the rate of inflation. The great deceleration in the rate of inflation led to a large increase in real tax revenue.

The effect described above came to be called in economic literature the "Tanzi effect" and, in Argentina, the "Tanzi-Oliveira effect" in recognition that Professor Julio Oliveira, an Argentine economist, had noticed the fall in tax revenue associated with high inflation. Mr. Oliveira had reported the fall but had not provided an explanation for it; instead he had focused on its implications for macroeconomic developments. The "Tanzi effect" was first described, in its technical details in the article "Inflation, Lags in Collection, and the Real Value of Tax Revenue" published in March 1977 in the Fund's academic journal, *IMF Staff Papers* and, in June 1977, in *Ensayos Económicos,* the economic journal of the Central Bank of Argentina. The article developed the theory and applied it to the concrete case of Argentina. An estimation of the average collection lag was provided. The article became one of the most cited papers written by Fund economists. It estimated a collection lag of 4.3 months in the Argentine tax system at that time. Given the size of this lag, it was easy to see why the acceleration of the inflation rate in 1975 and 1976 had caused such a large fall in the level of taxes. The relation between inflation and taxes had first been described in a report written by one of the missions that visited Argentina in 1976. The head of that mission, from the Western Hemisphere Department, had wanted to eliminate this part from the report because it did not conform to traditional Fund reports. Insistence from my own department kept it in.

The March 1977 article in the *IMF Staff Papers* attracted a lot of attention in Argentina and in other countries, because it clarified the relationship between inflation and tax revenue at a time when inflation was a big problem and was empirically important. However, the name given to it, "Tanzi effect," came later and, to this day, I have not been able to determine who first referred to it in this way. I would definitely send the person a nice gift. However, I distinctly recall the first time I heard the expression: It was the early 1980s and I was having lunch in the IMF building's dining room with Jeffrey Frankel, who is now a professor at the Harvard Kennedy School (at that time he was teaching in one of the California Universities). During the luncheon, he referred to the "Tanzi Effect" and, at first, I thought he was referring to a paper I had written in the mid-1970s amending the relationship between the rate of inflation and the nominal rate of interest. The so-called "Fisher effect," named after one of the most famous American economists of the first half of last century, Irving Fisher, had postulated that, in equilibrium, the nominal rate of interest would rise by the expected rate of inflation, thus leaving the real rate unchanged. If in a period of price stability the interest rate had been, say, 3 percent and people came to expect an inflation of 5 percent, then the nominal rate of interest would rise to about 8 percent.

In the mid-1970s, three papers written independently and published at approximately the same time had shown that, when there are income taxes, the "Fisher effect" no longer holds. I wrote one of these papers. The other two were written by Michael Darby and Martin Feldstein respectively. I had sent a copy of my yet unpublished paper to Milton Friedman, who sent me a nice letter in which he agreed with my analysis and noted his surprise at having received two other papers at about the same time, all making similar points but using different analyses. This amended "Fisher effect" came to be called in some publications the "Darby-Feldstein-Tanzi effect." But most referred to it as the "Darby effect," so Feldstein and Tanzi lost out on that one. Over lunch, I realized that Jeffrey Frankel was referring to my 1977 *Staff Paper* article and not to my earlier paper.

Because in the early 1980s inflation became a big problem in many countries, and the rate of inflation in Argentina would rise sharply again between 1980 and 1984, the "Tanzi effect" became probably the only effect in the history of economics that ended up in the daily newspapers and became known even to the taxi drivers of Buenos Aires. However, they thought that "efecto Tanzi" was the full name of a person who had something to do with inflation and taxes. At that time, finance ministers would frequently state their preoccupation about the "efecto Tanzi."

Recently, in 2004, I learned in an indirect and amusing manner just how popular the "Tanzi effect" had become in high-inflation countries. In the second half of 2003 I had resigned from my position as undersecretary in the Italian Ministry of Economy and Finance and joined the InterAmerican Development Bank (IDB) in Washington as a consultant. One day, I was introduced to one of the two vice presidents of the bank, Mr. Paulo Páiva, who had been minister of labor in Brazil. He seemed to be particularly pleased to meet me. He said that he had heard a lot about me and, in particular, I had been an important member of his family for over fifteen years. I was obviously very curious to discover why. He explained that in the mid-1980s, his young son had wanted a dog. The parents first resisted the idea because of the logistic difficulties that the dog would create. But in the end they gave in and bought one. The father wanted to name the dog after an economist because he wanted his son to become interested in economics. Thus, a natural name for the dog was Keynes. However, the boy had difficulty pronouncing Keynes and he did not like that name. So, after some discussion, the dog's name was changed to Tanzi because, at that time, the "Tanzi effect" was often mentioned in newspapers and, for Portuguese speakers, it was easy to pronounce. Thus for some fifteen years, Tanzi, the dog, was an important member of the Páiva family. However, the dog was never completely trained so, once in a while, he would do his business inside the house. In the Páiva family this became known as the "efecto Tanzi."

Several economic articles in the 1970s, some in top journals such as the *American Economic Review,* argued that a developing country that needed to build some infrastructure for growth, but could not raise enough tax money to pay for it, could resort to inflationary finance. In other words, it could have the central bank print more money to pay for the investment. At that time, the international financial market was still not very active in making foreign loans available and "private-public partnerships" in the building of infrastructure were still a thing of the future. Therefore, borrowing from the central bank looked like a good option, especially if one assumed that the positive impact on growth that came from the infrastructure more than compensated for the negative impact coming from higher inflation.

The problem with borrowing from the central bank is that it may create too much money and lead to high inflation. High inflation, as I had shown in my March 1977 article in the *IMF Staff Papers,* can lead to a fall in tax revenue. Consequently, if a country tries to finance public spending by printing more money, the act of printing more money, by increasing the rate of inflation, could reduce tax revenue by more than the real value of the income from inflationary finance (from the printing of money). In another article published in the September 1978 issue of the *IMF Staff Papers* called "Inflation, Real Tax Revenue, and the Case of Inflationary Finance: Theory with an

Application to Argentina," I worked out the theoretical underpinning of the basic relationships and applied the theory to the real case of Argentina. The basic variables in this analysis were: (a) the initial ratio of money to income; (b) the sensitivity of the demand for money to inflation; (c) the ratio of total tax revenue to national income at a zero inflation rate; and (d) the average collection lag for the tax system. It may be worthwhile to cite directly from the summary and conclusions of the article:

"The major conclusion that can be derived from the foregoing analysis is that, on the basis of realistic assumptions supported by empirical evidence, the existence of lags in tax collection implies that a government's gains from the use of inflationary finance are likely to be lower than has commonly been assumed. If the lags are long and the initial tax burden is high, the loss in (tax) revenue may be substantial, and it may neutralize any gain coming from central bank financing of the deficit.: Thus, a government would gain no extra revenue by relying on inflationary finance while the country would suffer the consequences of inflation."

The analysis of this paper and its basic model entered the economic literature although, unlike the "Tanzi effect" paper, its contributor was often omitted. It became a pure public good. In any case, I felt it made an important addition to our understanding of economic relations and may have prevented some major mistakes in economic policy.

These two papers had some impact on economic policy throughout the years when inflation remained high, say until the mid-1990s. Inspired by these papers, several countries tried to reduce the size of the collection lag in their tax systems and some, such as Brazil and Chile, went as far as indexing the tax liability for the rate of inflation so as to reduce or neutralize the impact of the collection lag on tax revenue. Of course, part of the fall in tax revenue may also have been due to delays in tax payments, beyond the collection lag, due to expectations of tax amnesties and to the high cost, or even unavailability, of credit from the banking systems.

CHAPTER IV

The Alfonsín Government and the "Lost Decade"

In the later part of the 1970s, the security situation got better and the members of the IMF missions felt more comfortable venturing out of the hotel for dinners and to visit other areas. The economic situation had also improved somewhat but not enough. The rate of inflation fell down from 444 percent in 1976, to 175 percent in 1978, and to around 100 percent in 1980; the fiscal deficit fell to around 5–6 percent of GDP, reflecting the increase in taxes and the contraction, at least up to 1979, in primary spending (i.e., public spending net of interest payments). Then, however, the situation started to deteriorate again. Public expenditure increased; inflation accelerated again, pushing down the tax revenue level; and the share of foreign debt into GDP went up rapidly. The latter was due to the greater availability of foreign loans, following the sharp increase in oil prices that created "petrodollars" looking for international investment opportunities. In 1978 I asked to be removed from the Argentine missions, so I did not follow closely the economic developments in Argentina for a few years.

In my last trip to Buenos Aires in late 1978, my mother insisted that I visit an old friend of hers whom she had grown up with in Italy and who had emigrated to Argentina with her husband in 1945. Over the years, they had occasionally exchanged a few letters, so my mother knew where her friend lived. I asked the personnel of the Central Bank if they could make arrangements for a car to take me to her house. We drove to what was obviously a relatively poor area of Buenos Aires and the car stopped at the address I had. I knocked on the door, which was opened by an elderly lady who seemed surprised and concerned by the presence of a stranger. I introduced myself and explained that I was bringing greetings from my mother. Her face lit up immediately and she invited me into her modest apartment. By this time, she lived alone, on a pension, because her husband had died some years earlier. She offered me a cup of coffee and inquired about my mother. While she prepared coffee, and then sat with me, she kept telling me how sorry she felt for the people she had left behind in Italy. She considered herself lucky for having left Italy immediately at the end of World War II, when that country was very poor and in ruins. She seemed to have no perception of how much Italy had changed from 1945 to 1978. During these years, the rich country, Argentina, had become relatively poor, and the poor country, Italy, had gone through a period of fast growth (the "Italian miracle"), which had transformed its economy making it, in time, one of the seven countries with the highest total income in the world. In some ways, fate had played a trick on many of those who left Italy in 1945 for the rich country that was Argentina.

I knew the relatives of this lady in Italy and knew that, by 1978, they were relatively well-off, earning incomes far above that of their Argentine relative. On the other hand, the old lady thought of them as living in the conditions that had prevailed at the very end of the highly destructive World War II. She had never gone back to Italy and she still considered herself the lucky one. I debated on whether I should tell her the truth or not but decided that, perhaps, it was better to keet quiet and simply inform her that her relatives in Italy were okay. However, I kept thinking that destiny had been cruel with many of the Italians who had emigrated to Argentina when, they thought, God was Argentine. I often thought about this visit, which made a big impact on me. Of course, I was also aware that many Argentines of Italian origin whom I had met and would continue to meet over the years, had done very well and were among the richest Argentines. For the masses, however, from a purely economic standpoint, it would have been better in the long run to remain in their country of origin. By 1978, many Argentines of Italian origin had started leaving Argentina and returning or emigrating to Italy, thus reversing the direction of the historical migratory flow. The fact that many Argentines of Italian descent had Italian passports, or could apply for them, facilitated this flow. Some left Argentina for political reasons, but many did it for economic reasons. Long lines started forming at Italian consulates in Argentina as the descendants of Italians applied for Italian passports.

In this last trip, some of the members of the IMF missions visited in the evenings or on the weekends the antique auction that took place at Patio Bullrich, before it was converted into a luxury shopping center. In the past, this building located in the heart of Buenos Aires was a place where cattle was auctioned. I have noticed over the years that when the economic situation of a country deteriorates seriously, the supply of antiques increases. I would see this phenomenon clearly in Eastern Europe in the early 1990s, and I had seen it in Portugal in January 1976. Families who run into financial difficulties usually start disposing of non-essential but valuable items they have acquired in more prosperous times. Many of the items being auctioned at Patio Bullrich had been bought by rich Argentines in Europe at the beginning of the century, when "God was Argentine" and their incomes were much higher than those of many Europeans. At that time, it was common for wealthy Argentines to go to Europe and come back with trunks full of items bought there. The fact that, then, travel was by boat facilitated the carrying of large numbers of items such as paintings, valuable glasses, statues, furniture, and so on. In a strange reversal of fortunes, many of those bidding for these objects were art dealers from Europe. I recall speaking to some of them who had come expressly from Florence for the antique auction at Patio Bullrich. The deteriorating economic situation and the devalued exchange rate made the auctioned items very attractive for these dealers. Thus, there was not only a change in the flow of emigration, but also in the flow of precious items that had come from Europe. I especially recall that French Galé glasses and Italian paintings did very well at the auction.

Up to that time, I had not paid much attention to the topic of corruption in Argentina or elsewhere. In later years, and especially in the 1990s, when the corruption scandal called "tangentopoli" led to the fall of the Italian government and the replacement of a whole political class, I would become very interested in the existence of corruption and in its implications in the performance of economies. In the 1990s, I would write several papers on this topic and play a significant role in the awakening of the IMF to its economic implications. During this 1978 mission, I met a former Argentine student of mine who lived in Buenos Aires. He was the son of a successful real estate entrepreneur. My former student, Armando, told me an interesting story that made me think about some aspects of corruption. He told me that his father had been approached by someone in the military with a specific proposal that I will describe.

In Buenos Aires at that time, and even today, some of the big avenues were one-way traffic. This meant that drivers could see, at street crossings, only the sides of the buildings facing them as they drove. These sides had acquired great rental value because they were used for displaying publicity. By the same token, the opposite sides had no value for drivers could not see them as they sped along the avenues. The high-ranking military official proposed that the father of my former student start renting the walls on the opposite sides of the buildings. He could do this at a very low cost because they were not considered valuable for attaching publicity. The military officer explained that, once the rental of these spaces was completed, he would change the direction of traffic. This change would dramatically increase the publicity rates of the rented walls for advertisers so my student's father would make a lot of money that he would share with the military man. I was told that the proposal was rejected by my student's father. This made me appreciate, perhaps for the first time, the power of regulations in eliciting bribes. Over future years, I would become progressively more aware of the existence of corruption in Argentina and, of course, in many other places, and of the role of regulations in this phenomenon. The story of the colonel's proposal had been a real eye opener.

I do not recall whether I went back to Argentina before the election of President Alfonsín of the Unión Cívica Radical on December 10, 1983. But I returned shortly after the election, and a few times while Alfonsín was president. After an interlude of a bit more than a year—during which Bernardo Grinspun was minister of economy and Enrique García Vázquez was president of the Central Bank—there were a few people in the new government that I knew well, including Mario Brodersohn, who had been a classmate of mine at Harvard, and Juan Carlos Gómez Sabaini, who had worked in the same office of the Joint Tax Program in Washington, where I had been a consultant until 1973. Brodersohn had become the finance secretary and Gómez Sabaini the revenue undersecretary. Brodersohn was an art collector and Gomez Sabaini was married to a prominent Argentine artist. They were both good friends and able individuals who hoped to make a difference in a period that, unfortunately, turned out to be disastrous from an economic point of view. It would end with the resignation of Alfonsín before his mandate expired. The Alfonsín period would accompany a further sharp fall in the Argentine people's standard of living.

The Alfonsín government, a democratically elected one after eight years of military interlude, came with big plans and big dreams. Alfonsín had great confidence in his ability to bring a change for the better after a disastrous decade. He truly felt he could restore Argentina to its comfortable past. One early dream that quickly vanished was to move the capital from Buenos Aires to a geographically more central location, as the Brazilians had done 25 years earlier. This would be one way of reducing the power of Buenos Aires and helping with the economic decentralization of Argentina.

Large areas of the country were still relatively empty while Buenos Aires had almost a third of the country's population and accounted for an even larger share of its total income. Another dream was to bring the economy under control with good policies and an honest administration. But, as someone once said, the trouble with dreams is that in the morning you wake up to reality. The reality was the disarray the new administration found and the limited power it had to do much about it. The war with the United Kingdom over the Islas Malvinas, or Falkland Islands, had been a political and economic disaster and the ongoing debt crisis in Latin America, which had started with the inability of Mexico to meet its debt obligations in 1982 did not help. The new administration inherited a house with a leaking roof in the middle of a storm.

In 1981 and 1982, the Argentine economy had contracted sharply at the rate of −6.2 percent in 1981 and −5.2 percent in 1982. It would recover a little in 1983, when it grew about 3 percent, but at the cost of a sharply accelerating inflation. The new government relied on the Keynesian recipe of fiscal expansion, but this produced high inflation and relatively little growth. The country's foreign debt had been increasing at a fast rate since 1978 and would reach high levels during the Alfonsín administration. Public spending had also gone up and so had the fiscal deficit, which by 1981–1982 had jumped to about 16 percent of GDP. The incidence of poverty, which had been low until the mid-1970s, had increased especially after 1980.

In 1980–1982, there was a large outflow of capital to the safe heaven offered by the United States, which allowed this money to earn tax free income in the banks where it was deposited and had become the major tax haven for rich Argentines. The attraction of safe and tax free rates of return in the United States at a time when, because of the Volcker attempt to kill inflation, real interest rates were very high, combined with problems in Argentina and the expectations of tax increases and lack of good opportunities for domestic investments, encouraged capital outflow. Tens of billions of dollars left Argentina. The 1980 capital flight had also much to do with a banking crisis that developed in a context of a fixed and highly overvalued exchange rate. In 1981, the capital flight was further stimulated by the Falkland war and the inflationary stampede with controlled interest rates.

In addition to my two friends, the new economic team in early 1985 included Juan Vital Sourrouille, as the economy minister, and José Luis Machinea as president of the Central Bank. Sourrouille and Machinea would become frequent visitors to the IMF in their attempts to negotiate programs of financial assistance. The new team tried hard to bring the crisis under control but in the end they were not successful, largely because they were unable to control the fiscal deficit. They experimented in 1985 with a heterodox plan, which included price controls, the "Plan Austral," and then again with a "Plan Primavera" in 1988. Both of these plans failed and the economy continued in its parlous and deteriorating state until 1989, when Alfonsín was forced out before the expiration of his mandate by spreading riots caused by sharply accelerating prices. In Argentina, spreading riots have occasionally led to changes in governments. Between 1975 and 1989, the share of public debt into GDP would rise from 14 to 66 percent with most of the increase happening during the Alfonsín period. But, of course, the balances held abroad by Argentine citizens also rose. In some indirect way, and especially during the 1979–1981 period, public borrowing abroad financed private capital outflow.

It is not possible to identify a single cause for the failure of the Alfonsín administration. Paraphrasing Tolstoy, "it is easier to tell why governments succeed than why they fail." But a few reasons can be mentioned.

First, the situation the Alfonsín administration inherited would have been a big challenge for any government. However, this explanation runs against the reality that, in 1989, the Menem government found perhaps an even worse domestic situation and, at least for a few years, was able to bring remarkable improvements to the economy and the fastest rate of growth that Argentina had for a long time. But, to be fair, the external environment was more favorable for Menem. The 1980s was a "lost decade" for Latin America and Argentina suffered the consequences of the debt crisis.

A second reason may have been that, from what I was told at the time, Alfonsín seemed to have no interest in, and no understanding of, economic matters. He was simply interested in "politics." He was the ultimate "político." When his ministers tried to discuss economic matters with him—and they tried hard—they would get his attention for only a very short time before he showed his boredom and shifted the discussion to what truly interested him: politics. He lived and practiced politics. He could not be bothered with trivial economic issues. One time, when he was told that there was a black market for dollars, he seemed surprised and tried to instruct his economic minister to pass a law to abolish it.

A third important reason is that the economic team seemed to have fallen prey to an Argentine habit: searching for a magical solution to a problem that could not be solved magically. Perhaps, the solution to Argentina's economic difficulties required a political power that the economic team did not have. But it also required a belief in traditional economic policies. The Alfonsín team continued to try heterodox measures combined with a firm belief that Keynesian fiscal stimulation would bring the economy out of the crisis. Unfortunately, they tried to apply the Keynesian recipe to an economy where the only financing the government had available to deal with the fiscal deficit was monetary expansion. The result was high inflation without any positive impact on the economy. The economic team also seemed to have accepted strange theories of inflation such as the belief that perishable staples with high seasonal price fluctuations were a major cause of rising prices. At that time, the price of beef was often blamed for inflation.

Rather than discuss the economic policies of the Alfonsín administration in detail, I will report on a couple of episodes.

Around 1985, Argentina had a program of financial assistance with the IMF. As was normal in those programs, the loans came with conditions attached to them. One of these conditions was that the size of the fiscal deficit should not exceed a given level. At that time, Argentina had great difficulties in meeting this fiscal ceiling, but without meeting it, it would not be able to continue receiving money from the Fund. Unable or unwilling to cut spending, the economic team was desperately in search of additional revenue. At that time, as the result of the famous real estate bubble in Japan, the price of real estate in Tokyo had gone through the roof. The value of the land in Tokyo was estimated to be higher than the value of all the land of the United States. This situation suggested a magical or practical, though unusual, solution to the fiscal difficulty of Argentina. Argentina could sell its embassy in Tokyo and use the proceeds from the sale to cover the fiscal gap. Argentina would then rent back the embassy from the new owner. In the Argentina team, there was an economist I had met at the Organization of American States when we both worked there. His name is Jorge Sakamoto, an Argentine of Japanese descent now living in Washington. He was the ideal person to negotiate the sale, so he was sent to Tokyo to conclude the deal. The sale went through and Argentina got revenue close to 0.5 percent of the Argentina GDP at that time. This revenue would help to fill the fiscal gap and keep the IMF happy and the money flowing in.

At that time, Argentina was in arrears with respect to some money it owed Japan. So, as a precaution, Sakamoto was instructed not to deposit the check at the Bank of Tokyo for fear that the money would not be transferred to Buenos Aires. This created some diplomatic difficulties and embarrassment on the part of the president of the bank, who took this as a personal affront. In any case, the transaction went through, the Argentine government got its money, and Sakamoto returned to Buenos Aires after concluding the successful deal. A few days after his return, he had to catch a taxi and the taxi driver, encouraged by Sakamoto's Japanese look, started to complain to him about the crooks in the Argentine government who were ruining the country. "Imagine," the taxi driver said, "they have even sold the Argentine embassy in Tokyo!" I am told that Sakamoto, who has a good sense of humor, was highly amused by this comment. Of course, the men in the streets also wondered whether the money ever made it into the country.

The sale of the embassy in Tokyo happened at about the same time when Mobutu, the then Congolese dictator, in order to comply with the fiscal requirements of a financial program with the Fund, which also required that the fiscal deficit be kept below a certain level, had the brilliant idea of selling his personal plane. He used the money to raise the country's revenue and then leased the plane right back. Again, the Fund was happy that the fiscal ceiling was respected and Mobutu complied with the conditions of the loan and continued to receive Fund money.

These and similar episodes made me start worrying seriously about the relationship between structural reforms and macroeconomic adjustment, and about the quality of fiscal policy. In the early 1980s, the Reagan administration had developed a strong interest in the supply side of the economy and in the factors, such as high marginal tax rates, that might constrain its growth. Robert Mundell had given academic backing to this line of thinking, while Arthur Laffer made it popular with his famous napkin example that introduced the "Laffer curve." Obviously, there should be a relationship between structural policies and the response of the supply side of the economy. This relationship must in time lead to macro-economic consequences.

After the long Keynesian interlude, in which all the attention of policy had gone to the demand side of the economy, it started to be appreciated that structural impediments could reduce the performance of an economy, regardless of the demand. This was perhaps the greatest contribution to economics that came from Reagan's presidency. It was almost a revolution. I felt that reducing the fiscal deficit in the way it was done in Argentina and the Congo (among many other examples), was not a desirable or acceptable policy or one that the IMF should approve. This argument did not seem to impress many of my colleagues at the Fund. Many of those who negotiated the Fund programs with the countries, especially those in the geographic or area departments, had a purely accounting, short-term, and legalistic view of fiscal conditionality so that, if a fiscal deficit was contained within the agreed limits during a relevant period, no matter how, this was good enough. This was consistent with the macro model that the Fund had been following over the years, which was based on a relation between the fiscal deficit and monetary expansion in the short run.

I was inspired to write a paper with the title "Fiscal Policy, Growth, and Design of Stabilization Programs." In this paper I argued that ". . . when a fiscal deficit needs to be reduced substantially, so that a country's economy can be stabilized, it is important that the deficit reduction be associated with *good* and *sustainable* tax and expenditure policies, rather than with poor and temporary policies. A stabilization program achieved through inefficient measures, or through measures that will not last over time, is likely to be disappointing." This paper was first presented and discussed in 1985, at one of the rare retreats that the managing directors of the Fund hold with Fund directors. At the time, the managing director was Jacques de Larosiére. The retreat was held in Annapolis, Maryland, and my paper was discussed, formally, by a French economist, Patrick de Fontenay, and then by the whole group of participants. To say that the reaction to the paper was cold would be the understatement of the year. Questions were raised about how much we at the Fund knew about structural policies; about interference in the internal political decisions of the countries; about the separation of the work of the Fund from that of the World Bank; about why it made a difference for the implicit Fund model (based on work by Jacques Polak, the former Fund's director of research), whether a fiscal ceiling, agreed between the IMF and a country's authorities, was met by selling an embassy or a plane or by making a permanent expenditure or tax change.

In spite of the initial cold reaction at the retreat, that paper helped to set in motion important changes in the work of the Fund that, as often happened, in time would take the Fund too much in the opposite direction. The program with Indonesia during the South East

Asia crisis in 1997–1998, for example, would have an extraordinary large number of "conditions." The paper had emphasized that "the impact of changes in fiscal deficits on economic objectives depends, to a considerable extent, on the quality of the specific measures employed." Interestingly, two decades later, the European Commission has discovered the importance of the *quality* of the specific measures employed. The Commission has been worried by the maneuvers of members of the European Monetary Union to circumvent the spirit of the Stability and Growth Pact (SGP) through financial engineering and *una tantum* measures. European countries have been using measures similar to those described twenty years earlier in my paper to stay under the 3 percent deficit ceiling required by the SGP. In some cases, European countries have sold the buildings that house the ministries to get revenue and rented them right back. This way, they could claim to keep their fiscal deficits under the ceiling set by the Pact. There is a close parallel between recent developments in the European Union with respect to the SGP and developments under IMF programs. History tends to repeat itself.

My paper was presented again at a seminar sponsored by the IMF and the Instituto Torcuato di Tella, then an Argentine think tank and now a university. The seminar was held in Buenos Aires on October 13–16, 1986 and the papers presented were published in a book edited by Ana María Martirena-Mantel, an Argentine economist. The title of the book was *External Debt, Savings, and Growth in Latin America* (Washington, D.C.: The Fund; Buenos Aires: Instituto Di Tella, 1987). The seminar was attended by several important economists, including the late Rudi Dornbusch, and by some economists now holding important positions in Latin American countries such as Vittorio Corbo (president of the Central Bank of Chile) and Guillermo Ortiz (president of the Central Bank of Mexico). The two discussants of my paper were Luis Jorge Garay S. from Colombia and Ricardo Hausmann from Venezuela. Hausmann, now a Professor at the Harvard Kennedy School, stressed the fact that the approach suggested in my paper required a longer-run perspective than the one then followed by the IMF, and a clearer definitions of the responsibilities of the World Bank and the IMF. Where the responsibilities of the Bank ended and those of the Fund started had been a contentious question over the years and would become even more so as each institution, because of what was called "mission creep," stepped in the areas of the other. This was in a way inevitable, because it makes little sense to compartmentalize the economic areas of responsibility as the two institutions' mandates tried to do. Both discussants stated that the proposed approach conflicted with the traditional Fund programs. The paper was republished in my book *Public Finance in Developing Countries* (Elgar Pub, 1991).

The paper was influential in awakening the Fund to the fact that worrying strictly about the size of the fiscal deficit, without putting it in a structural and longer-term context, was not very useful. It meant that adjustment often lasted only as long as a country had a program with the Fund. This problem would reappear with a vengeance some years later in transition economies, prompting me to write another paper also published in the *IMF Staff Papers* (vol. 40, no. 4, 1993) warning about the interpretation of the fiscal deficit in transition countries. What was frustrating was that many economists, trained mainly as macroeconomists, often failed to appreciate the importance of the issues I was discussing. Some of these economists occupied at times very high positions in the IMF. The fact that only now the European Commission has discovered the importance of the quality of the fiscal adjustment indicates that this problem was not confined to the IMF.

I went back to Buenos Aires in 1987, although I do not recall the precise date. In those years, I attended a few conferences held outside of Buenos Aires. In the 1987 trip, I was accompanied by the late Carlos Aguirre, a Uruguayan who, at that time, was the chief of the tax administration division in the Fiscal Affairs Department. We had been invited to assess some current developments in the tax administration of Argentina, the Direccion General Impositiva (DGI). A new tax administrator had been appointed head of the DGI. He had come from one of the big accounting firms and was part of the political group ("La Coordinadora"), which coordinated policies for the Alfonsín administration. This man had political standing; he was not a tax expert but a manager, one who, we were told, would know how to reorganize the tax administration.

When we visited the office of the new director, we met an enthusiastic young man who explained to us that he had bought some computers from the French government with which he was going to improve the performance of the tax administration. He claimed that he already had a great deal of information on taxpayers stored in the computers' memory. As a demonstration, we asked him to insert the name of a typical Argentine enterprise to see the kind of information he could reproduce. It soon became clear to us that this was the latest attempt at trying to find a magical solution to the tax administration's problems. In this case, an instrument (computers) was bought at a high cost before knowing what to do with it. Somehow, there was the hope that the instrument would itself suggest the solution. We had seen this approach in other countries, especially at that time when the use of computers was spreading. Smart computer salesmen were convincing gullible public servants that computers could somehow produce instant miracles. But, at best, computers allowed tax administrations to perform more quickly the inefficient operations that they had been performing manually. The GIGO principle was clearly valid—garbage in, garbage out. Only in later years, when procedures were straightened and careful assessments of how computers could be used for storing information and for retrieving it were made, they began to be useful and, in some countries, to even make a difference in the administration of the tax system.

I recall that the day when we left Buenos Aires was very windy. That night we would leave for Miami, where we would change planes for Washington, D.C. About one hour after the plane took off, it started bouncing up and down and there was frequent lightning around it. The pilot informed the passengers that the plane was trying to make its way between two huge storms and that he could not avoid the turbulence; the storms were so large that he could not go around them either. We sat back in one of the most frightening experiences one can have. The plane was bouncing and creaking so much that I was afraid that, at some point, it would just disintegrate. The lightning around it added to the feeling of terror. It was so intense that it felt like being in the middle of the 4th of July fireworks. I kept wondering what a lightning hit could do to a plane and did not have an answer. The turbulence lasted about half an hour but it felt like an eternity. I came to appreciate Einstein's definition of relativity: "If you are in the company of a pretty young lady for two hours, it feels like two minutes. If you have your foot in a brace for two minutes it will feel like an eternity. That is relativity."

CHAPTER V

The First Menem Administration

By 1989, the economic situation in Argentina had deteriorated dramatically. The per capita income had fallen well below the level reached twenty years earlier. This was the end of a period that would go from 1975 to 1990 and see the per capita income fall by about 25 percent. Some economists would characterize these fifteen years as one of the real depressions of the twentieth century. In both 1988 and 1989, the growth rate had been sharply negative. The rate of inflation had risen to almost 400 percent in 1988, and to a hyperinflationary level of almost 5000 percent per year in 1989. Unemployment was sharply up and real wages sharply down. There were widespread riots caused by the increase in prices. The year 1989 saw the end of the Alfonsín government and the beginning (on July 8) of the Menem administration, which would last for ten years. Like Perón's, the Menem administration would start triumphantly and end less well, but democratically, and Menem would complete a second term. Public finances would again play a major role in this deterioration.

At the time of Menem's election in May 1989, I had traveled to Argentina to speak at a conference in the province of Santa Fe in honor of Raúl Prebisch. Prebisch had been an Argentine economist and minister of economy, who after World War II, was very influential in Latin American countries. He had been the leading advocate of policies of import substitution through which, he hoped, Latin America would become an industrialized region. This would thus reduce its dependence on the exportation of commodities whose prices he and other economists of the so-called "structuralist school" believed tended to fall historically. Prebisch's ideas had found a powerful base in the UN's Economic Commission for Latin America, headquartered in Santiago, Chile, of which he had become the executive secretary.

The Conference in Santa Fe took place in the middle of a raging inflation that was moving fast toward hyperinflation, a situation in which money loses its value completely. At the time of the conference, money still retained some value but that value was falling by the hour: People shopping at supermarkets would at times experience price increases of as much as 20 percent from the time they entered a cashier's line to the time they had to pay for their purchases. Loudspeakers would announce the increases in the prices that would become effective at a specific moment. At this rate of inflation, prices tend to become greatly distorted because the increases cannot be synchronized. The cost of the hotel room in Santa Fe, at the nice hotel where the conference was being held, was only $20 (U.S. dollars) at the black market rate and one could buy a pair of shoes for $5 (U.S. dollars).

The Prebisch Conference, opened by Víctor Hipólito Martínez, the vice president of Argentina between 1983 and 1989, was not particularly interesting. There were the usual arguments that the country's economic problems came from the low prices that industrial countries paid for the commodities they bought from Argentina. This followed a common Argentine trait of attributing domestic problems to foreigners. By this time, Argentina was clearly in the group of developing countries, having made the backward transition from its earlier position as one of the richest countries in the world. After the conference, I was interviewed on television with Marcelo Lascano, an Argentine economist, and asked to give the definition of hyperinflation. Was the current level of inflation in Argentina hyperinflation? I answered that when the increase in prices reaches 5000 per year, that question becomes a semantic one; one can define it as one wishes but clearly inflation has become a big problem. I was also asked whether it would be possible to replace all taxes with a single tax on transactions, an idea that was gaining currency at the time.

In late August 1989, the International Institute of Public Finance (IIPF) was going to hold its annual congress in Buenos Aires and the nominating committee had recommended that I be elected the next president. The current president of the IIPF had been considering whether to cancel the congress in view of the public disorder and the price rises in Argentina, events that were widely reported by the international press. In consultation with Professor Ernesto Rezk of the province of Córdoba, who was the chairman of the local organizing committee, I argued against canceling the congress on the grounds that Buenos Aires would be safe. The local committee had worked hard to make the practical arrangements for a successful congress.

Before returning to Washington after the Prebisch Conference, I was contacted by Guido di Tella and Rodolfo Frigeri, two members of the Menem team, to discuss the possibility of the IMF assisting the new government that would be taking over in a few weeks, with the reform of the tax system and the tax administration. They indicated that the government needed to raise the level of taxation. They were also concerned about widespread corruption and absenteeism in the tax administration. We agreed that a tax mission, that I would probably lead, would come to Buenos Aires to complete its work before the meeting of the International Institute of Public Finance, toward the end of August, which I was attending. Guido di Tella would in time become the Argentine ambassador to Washington and, later, the minister of foreign affairs. He belonged to a distinguished family of industrialists of Italian background that had created a well-known think-tank called the Torcuato di Tella Institute. Rodolfo Frigeri would become finance secretary and, successively, president of the Banco Provincia de Buenos Aires. Over the following years, I would be in touch with them often.

During this visit, Frigeri invited me to attend with him and his wife the annual event called "Exposición Rural," organized by the Argentine association of agricultural producers. This is the occasion when the agricultural sector of Argentina shows off the magnificent animals it produces. These are the animals that generate the fabled Argentine meat. The event, half fair and half circus, takes place in a large stadium in Buenos Aires and is attended by tens of thousands of people, especially on opening day when the presentation of the prized animals is made and the circus-like,or spectacular part of the event is most important. It starts with the parade of truly impressive samples of cows, bulls, pigs, horses, and so on; all of which have won prizes and are worth great sums of money, and ends with equestrian games requiring exceptional skills. I had never seen samples of cattle of this size or the skills displayed in the equestrian games and I enjoyed the show a immensely. This was one of the most interesting and visually attractive spectacles I had ever seen and would strongly recommend it to anyone. It should be in every tourist guide of Argentina.

However, the real attraction that year was the participation of the newly elected and charismatic president, Carlos Menem. Menem, an Argentine of Syrian descent, in a country where Syrian is synonymous with rich, had been the governor of a small and poor province, La Rioja. He had been notorious for the large number of people who were given (provincial) government jobs in his province. He represented the return of the Peronists to power after 1976. Menem entered the stadium in an open golden Cadillac convertible, the type that was common in the 1960s, when cars seemed as long as luxury liners. The car made the round of the stadium moving slowly while Menem, standing, blew kisses to the crowd. The enthusiasm of the crowd was contagious and overwhelming. I could easily imagine a Roman emperor making the round of the Coliseum on a chariot; or a toreador making the round of a Madrid stadium after a successful *corrida*. It was clear that Menem had a special charisma and that he knew how to relate to the crowd. At this abysmal time in Argentinean history, in the middle of a hyperinflation and after many years of negative growth rates, he must have been seen by the crowd as a potential savior, and Argentina badly needed a savior.

Menem would surprise the political establishment with several of his appointments, as he clearly tried to reach out to various political forces. He was street smart, quick, and decisive. He would impress the people who worked for him with his ability to grasp issues and make quick decisions. He tried to reach out beyond the "compañeros," i.e., the true Peronists. In one case, he offered someone from the opposition a high position in his administration. The person contacted revealed, with full honesty, that he had not voted for him, but Menem replied that it did not matter because he was sure that next time he would vote for him. One individual who was invited to join the new administration and who would play a very important role in it was Domingo Cavallo. Menem invited him to be the minister of foreign affairs, not an obvious position for someone with a Ph.D. in economics. Cavallo was an influential economist who had been president of the Central Bank briefly in the early 1980s and the head of Fundación Mediterranea, a think tank in the province of Córdoba. He had received his Ph.D. in economics from Harvard and, like many Argentines, was of Italian background.

I returned to Washington to prepare for the tax mission and for the IIPF meeting in Buenos Aires. The mission that went to Buenos Aires in August was, by Fund standards, a high-powered one which included Milka Casanegra, the head of the Tax Administration Division in the Fiscal Affairs Department at the IMF, and who had been, for a while, director of taxation in Chile; Mario Blejer, who years later would become president of Argentina's Central Bank: Carlos Silvani, who would later become Argentina's director of taxation and revenue secretary, and myself. The World Bank decided to add an Italian, Luca Barbone, to the mission. The mission was a bit unusual because it included two Argentine nationals and a Chilean, a nationality not popular in Argentina.

When we arrived in Buenos Aires, we were faced with the following situation: The overall tax to GDP ratio for the whole public sector had fallen dramatically, in part as a result of the high rate of inflation. The authorities were anxious to go to Congress in September with proposals for a fundamental reform of the tax system. However, they had not made up their mind about what to propose. Political divisions within the economic team (between traditional Peronists and those who had come from the private sector, including the minister of economy), plus the fact that at least five different groups, all reflecting particular political and economic interests, were pushing for their own pet ideas did not make the task easy. Some would propose tinkering with the present system without fundamental reform. Others would push for radical and never-tested changes such as replacing all taxes with a single one. Others would push for more tax incentives in a country that was drowning in tax incentives. The search for the magical formula was clearly on. This search was a constant in Argentina and in some other Latin American countries. A committee of tax "notables," mostly tax consultants to the private sector, had been created to discuss alternatives but had not been able to reach a decision. Because of the frequent turnover at the top of the tax administration several of these notables had been directors of taxation.

After analyzing the alternatives proposed, we concluded that none of them would meet the needed objectives, namely: to (a) raise the tax ratio, (b) simplify the system and give it more transparency, (c) reduce evasion, and (d) remove, or at least significantly reduce, the distortions and the disincentive effects of the present system. At this point, we were faced with the double problem of developing alternative proposals and "selling" them in the most diplomatic way to the government. This task was not made easy by the fact that one alternative set of proposals (made by the Bunge y Born group, a powerful Argentine multinational company) had the implicit sponsorship of the minister and vice minister of economy, who had come from the group sponsoring this alternative. This group, as it would be expected, pushed for more tax incentives. Another alternative set (that of the Fundación Mediterranea) had the implicit sponsorship of Domingo Cavallo, the minister of foreign affairs. This group was pushing an idea, developed in a paper by Aldo Dadone, to replace all taxes with a single tax on transactions. It was claimed that such a tax would generate more revenue than the current system.

After considerable discussion among ourselves, we came up with a tax reform package based on best practices that included, broadly, the following proposals:

For the taxation of consumption or sales: replace the existing taxes by (a) a generalized, broad-based value-added tax with a single rate. This change would considerably expand revenue because, at that time, 49 percent of the tax base of the value-added tax was legally exempt while the remaining 51 percent evaded the tax with considerable facility; (b) excise taxes on only four groups of products: tobacco, alcoholic beverages, soft drinks, and petroleum products. This change would eliminate many existing taxes that generated almost no revenue while they absorbed considerable administrative resources. The proposed taxes could be justified on the basis of benefit received or negative externalities generated.

For taxes on foreign trade: (a) eliminate the taxes on exports; (b) remove the existing quantitative restrictions on imports and replace them by tariffs; in a process referred to as tariffication; (c) over a four year period, reduce all high import tariffs to a rate not to exceed 20 percent; and (d) put immediately a *minimum* tax on all imports. The minimum tax should be 10 percent at the beginning and should progressively be raised to the level of the uniform rate. Such a minimum tax could raise substantial revenue because almost half of all imports came in duty free and some at duties of less than 10 percent. It would also reduce differences in what economists call effective protection.

For taxes on the incomes of individuals: (a) broaden the base of the tax by eliminating most deductions and by lowering the personal exemption that was exceptionally large in relation to the per capita income of Argentina, thus legally exempting much of the income from the tax base; (b) raise the first rate to 10 percent and tax higher incomes at marginal rates of 20 percent and 30 percent; (c) rely on final withholding taxes on payments of interests and dividends. At that time the taxes on the incomes of individuals generated very little revenue; thus, they provided a potentially important tax base.

For taxes on enterprise incomes: the mission proposed the elimination of the taxes on corporate income and on net wealth and their replacement by a tax on the gross assets of the enterprises. This was a new kind of tax originally proposed by Maurice Allais, a Nobel-prize winning French economist, and first introduced in Mexico by Francisco Gil-Diaz, the tax director who would later become minister of finance. The reasons for this radical proposal were two: First, the two taxes that would be replaced had generated very little revenue in recent years. Second, the macroeconomic turmoil had caused the enterprises to accumulate enormous deductible paper losses, which guaranteed that they would hardly pay any taxes for many years to come under the current system.

We also stressed that no tax reform would achieve much if the existing tax incentive legislation, which had become a cancer in the Argentine tax system, was not abolished or at least replaced by direct subsidies; and if the Dirección General Impositiva (the tax administration) was not reformed to reduce corruption and inefficiency. We made some recommendations aimed at this latter objective and proposed that a later mission would deal more specifically with it. We estimated that the proposed changes, if fully implemented and well administered, would raise the level of taxation to about 24 percent of GDP that would be a historical high. Specifically, we estimated that the value-added tax could generate 6 percent of GDP, a figure that was three times as large as the current figure and that was ridiculed by some Argentine experts. We stressed that the 24 percent of GDP level could be achieved only if the inflation rate came down.

The proposals of the IMF mission were explained to the relevant authorities and, at the request of President Menem, were then presented, at a marathon meeting that lasted two full days in a secluded area outside of Buenos Aires, to the 22 experts that formed the tax commission that had unsuccessfully tried to develop an agreed package. The proposals were explained and discussed. The experts, who for the most part worked as tax consultants to taxpayers, including enterprises, were concerned that the proposals would simplify the Argentine tax system to such an extent that they would find themselves without work. Nevertheless, after considerable debate, at times very heated, in the end the tax proposals were endorsed by the group. This was a great achievement for the mission. We felt that we had almost succeeded in a "mission impossible."

On my return to our hotel in Buenos Aires after the meeting, I was contacted by someone who claimed to be a relative of President Menem. The man said he wanted to talk to me. He came accompanied by two other people, who said they were members of parliament, and tried to convince me of the merits of the magical solution of a single tax. This man truly believed that a single tax on all transactions could magically eliminate administrative problems and tax evasion, maintain economic incentives, and generate the level of taxes that Argentina needed. I listened politely telling this individual that his interesting idea would be studied carefully. In my many years of work in this field, I was repeatedly amazed and amused by the number of people who believed that they had found the magical solution to the tax problem. These people were never genuine tax experts. Perhaps, once one becomes a true expert, one loses his or her imagination. This activity is similar to that of the alchemists in their attempts to produce gold out of lead. The current campaign in many countries for a flat rate income tax may be the latest version of this search for the magical formula.

I was invited to meet President Menem at the Casa Rosada, the official office of the President. I went to see him accompanied by Mr. Rapanelli, the economy minister. Menem received me warmly and showed great interest in the work of the mission and thanked me and the Fund for it. He asked many questions about our proposals and made strong statements about the need to find a permanent solution to Argentina's fiscal problem. I stressed that without a solution to this problem no sustainable improvement would be possible for the Argentine economy and that such a solution would need to involve both raising revenue *and* reducing expenditure. I was with him for about one hour and, by the time I left, he had made me feel as if we had known each other for years. I very much appreciated this quality of his personality, which obviously helped him be a successful politician. He could not have been friendlier.

In later years, I recalled this meeting when I heard a story involving Menem and Enrique Iglesias, the long-time president of the InterAmerican Development Bank, who retired from the Bank in October 2005. When Iglesias first met Menem, he naturally addressed him as "Presidente." Menem corrected him and asked him to call him Carlitos. Iglesias ignored the invitation and continued to call him "Presidente." Menem corrected him again, and asked to be called Carlitos. When this happened again, Iglesias is reported to have said that he could never call President Menem "Carlitos," but would reluctantly call him "Carlos."

As was mentioned above, Mr. Rapanelli, the minister of economy, had accompanied me to visit President Menem. Rapanelli had come from the multinational company Bunge y Born, a huge enterprise that traded in agricultural commodities and which had lent several senior individuals to Menem's first government. Rapanelli was a tall and pleasant individual. When we came out of the Casa Rosada, we were surrounded, or better mobbed, by a tidal wave of reporters who wanted some statement from us. Obviously, tax reform was a hot subject in Argentina. The minister told the reporters that a major reform of the tax system would be on the way.

The next day, a Sunday, my photo covered half of the front page of *La Nación*, one of Argentina's major newspapers. The article reported an interview I had had the night before with reporters from that newspaper, in which I had outlined in broad terms some of the main elements of the tax reform that we might propose. I recall that it was a beautiful, sunny day in early Argentine spring and that many individuals were outside, sitting in parks or in front of coffee shops. I had the feeling that everyone was reading *La Nación* and looking at me. I experienced how bad it must feel to lose your privacy and know that, wherever you go, people can recognize you. I tried to hide my identity behind sunglasses. I told myself that I would never wish to become a face everyone could recognize. But one problem that I could not avoid was the number of telephone calls I got at the hotel from radio stations and newspapers who wanted interviews. These calls did not seem to respect the hours of the day and would come very late at night and very early in the morning. So I instructed the hotel not to transfer calls to my room any longer. This of course created other problems.

Under normal circumstances, I would have left Buenos Aires the evening after the meeting with President Menem. However, the meeting of the IIPF would start on that Sunday and, because I was the person proposed to be the next president, I had to attend the meeting and, therefore, remain in Buenos Aires for four additional days until the end of the meeting. At that Monday's meeting of the Institute, I was elected the next president, a position that I would normally hold for three years. However, because of the cancellation of a congress that was to be held in Leningrad in 1991, I held the position for four years. The fact that I remained in Buenos Aires for four more days allowed me to follow some developments related to the tax reform.

During those four days the Council of Ministers met and endorsed the proposals of the IMF mission. Unfortunately, Menem did not participate in that meeting, presumably because he had been preparing for an official visit to Yugoslavia. He may have intentionally missed the meeting to retain more freedom of action. During those days, there were various comments in newspapers on the report of the mission which, as was common in Argentina (and in many other places), had been leaked to the press. There were no frontal attacks on the proposals, which were generally supported or even praised. But something similar to the probing of the walls that protected cities in medieval time against enemy forces started. One newspaper ran an editorial that addressed the proposal for a broad-based, no exclusion-allowed, value-added tax. The editorial praised the proposal declaring that it endorsed it, provided that there was one exception. The exception, naturally, was newspapers. The argument was that newspapers provide information necessary to the public; therefore, they must have special treatment. Another newspaper carried an article written by someone from the association of pharmaceutical products arguing that medicines are essential and cannot be taxed. These attacks convinced me of the merit of no exception in the value-added tax. Once an exception is provided for one product, there are many other products that can demand similar lenient treatment. Other articles tried to make the case for retaining incentives for poor regions.

The tax on gross assets was criticized by some because it might tax enterprises that "never made any profits." The question of how these enterprises had remained in operation without ever making any profits, and whether they should remain in existence if they did not make profits, was not asked. There were, of course, also some complaints against the proposal to reduce import duties to 20 percent. It was asked whether this would not drive some local producers, who had survived behind the high tariff walls, out of business. And what about the impact on employment? Also, the proposal to impose minimum taxes on imports that had been coming in duty free received some negative comments.

These comments that kept appearing in newspaper articles or were reported on the radio made me somewhat concerned about what would happen at the stage when the broad proposals of the IMF mission were drafted into specific laws, a process that in my experience always brings surprises; or when the drafted laws were sent to parliament for approval. These are the moments when the devil, who has been patiently lurking in the shadows, would attempt to get into the details and derail the reform. Obviously every public interest would use whatever power it had to get its preferred change to the proposals.

I got mixed signals from Menem himself after my meeting with him. The day before his departure for Yugoslavia, he gave a speech to industrialists in which he broadly supported the Fund proposals, but in his specifics he mentioned the changes that would reduce taxes but omitted those that would raise taxes. For example, he mentioned the elimination of export duties and the elimination of the taxes on the income and net wealth of enterprises, but he failed to mention the introduction of the minimum tax on imports and the tax on the gross assets of enterprises. There were probably political reasons for that, but I would have preferred that both positive and negative aspects had been mentioned at the same time. This, in fact, was a common problem for Fund technical missions. The government would often follow the painless advice but ignore the painful one and still argue that they had complied with many of the Fund's recommendations. This was made possible by the fact that Fund reports normally contained several recommendations and it was often possible for the countries' authorities to pick and choose. At the time, it was impossible to guess how many accommodations the government would make to the pressures from vested interests. These accommodations could come first in the drafting of the laws to be sent to parliament and, next, in the process of approval by parliament. It would have been naïve to expect the final product to have a close resemblance to the mission's proposals, but we hoped that the resemblance would still be there so that we would recognize and be willing to adopt the final product.

By December 1989, the Argentine parliament had approved a major reform of the Argentine tax system which bore close similarity to the proposals of the IMF mission. The tax on the net worth of enterprises was abolished and the tax on gross assets was introduced, but it was changed into a minimum tax to qualify as an income tax in the United States. Without such a qualification, American companies would not be able to rebate the tax paid in Argentina against their U.S. liabilities, because the U.S. would not recognize the gross asset tax as a tax on income. This was an example of the many ways in which the U.S. has influenced policy decision, especially in the area of taxation, in Latin American countries. The tax on the income of individuals was introduced with a minimum rate of 10 percent and a maximum rate of 30 percent, as proposed by the mission. The base for the value-added tax was widened, as proposed by the mission, but several products were given special treatment against the advice of the IMF mission. In spite of these differences, and with the continuing flirtation with magical solutions, such as consideration of a cash flow tax, and a tax on checks, the fiscal situation started improving.

The Fiscal Affairs Department of the IMF continued to provide assistance, especially in reforming the tax administration. A no-nonsense head of the tax administration, Ricardo Cosio, attempted to raise the performance of that institution. He would soon be accompanied by a rather formidable revenue secretary, Carlos Tacchi, in the attempt to raise tax revenue.

Two important administrative changes were made in the early 1990s. One was introduced at the recommendation of the IMF and especially of Carlos Silvani. The second one was pushed by Carlos Tacchi. The first was a strategy related to a Large Taxpayer Unit (LTU); the second was a widespread system of tax withholding. Both of these helped improve tax collection.

The strategy associated with the large taxpayer unit was the following: In the past, all enterprises or taxpayers had been treated equally and had received, at least in intention, the same attention. However, the statistics on taxpayers in most countries indicate that often a relatively small proportion of taxpayers (enterprises or individuals) pays the overwhelming proportion of income and value-added taxes. Thus, the strategy was to allocate the supervision of these large taxpayers to a specialized unit. This unit, the LTU, would develop effective systems of controls and monitoring of these taxpayers to make sure that they would report their incomes and sales accurately and on time, and make the payments when due. Computer programs would be developed for this purpose. Initially, this strategy, and the accompanying systems of control, would be applied to a fixed number, say the top 100 taxpayers. Such large taxpayers units exist in many countries. However, the Fund's strategy was that once the new systems of control were developed for these large taxpayers, and were shown to be effective, they would be applied to progressively larger groups so that, in time, these systems would cover most relevant taxpayers. In Argentina, the system worked in the initial phase of the strategy. The LTU was created, it dealt with the largest taxpayers, and the number of taxpayers was widened somewhat. However, the second phase of extending the systems developed to larger groups of taxpayers did not work as well as it was hoped. It is not clear whether the strategy was at fault or whether the administrators did not push hard enough for it.

Carlos Tacchi, the revenue secretary until 1995, was a firm believer that one way of controlling tax evasion was through a system of withholding of estimated taxes. Thus, whenever goods were imported or payments were made by the government or by large enterprises for goods purchased or for incomes paid, a deposit would be made based on the estimation of the tax that the transaction would eventually be associated with. These withholding of deposits could be claimed by the taxpayers at the end of the fiscal year, when final tax declarations were presented. This system proved effective but it inevitably created a lot of administrative costs and complications. The tax administration experts at the Fund were less favorable to it than Carlos Tacchi. However, some countries copied some of its features.

In 1992, I saw President Menem briefly in Washington, D.C., at a reception given for him at the Argentine Embassy. My wife and I had been invited and, upon arrival at the embassy, near Dupont Circle, we left the car with the valet at the entrance. The building was very crowded and President Menem, with his perennial suntan and long sideburns, was welcoming each guest as they came in, and kissing each one of the ladies. My wife was of course charmed by this gesture. Sometime later, Vice President Quayle arrived as the representative of the American administration. By this time, Menem was a hero for the U.S. Republican administration because of his market-oriented policies and, especially, because of the privatization program that he was pursuing. He was the center of attention at the reception and his charm was put to good use.

After a while, my wife and I decided to leave and went down to ask the young valets for our car. While we waited, a large demonstration suddenly materialized in front of the embassy. There must have been several hundred people carrying signs and chanting slogans. They had appeared out of nowhere. It turned out that the demonstration was not directed against Menem but against Vice President Quayle. The demonstrators were gay and were reacting against a speech Quayle had made that day in which he criticized the gay population. At that time, vice presidents were escorted by only a handful of secret service personnel compared to the army that now seems to accompany Vice President Cheney whenever he goes. Thus, the secret service agents were badly outnumbered by the progressively more excited gay protesters. Because we were waiting for our car at the entrance of the embassy, we were caught right in the middle. The secret service agents called for reinforcement and pulled their weapons. We were really scared and, for a while, thought that the whole situation could deteriorate into something ugly and dangerous. Fortunately, soon additional agents arrived and the demonstrators retreated while they continued singing about gay pride and chanting slogans against the vice president. We were happy to be able to get into our car and drive away.

CHAPTER VI

Predicting a Storm When the Sky Is Blue

and the Sun Is Shining

I went back to Buenos Aires in December 1992 for a brief visit accompanied by Partho Shome, an Indian economist who had often accompanied me in IMF missions. We had been invited by Domingo Cavallo, who was the minister of economy then. On April 1, 1991, Cavallo had introduced the "convertibility system," which had fixed the exchange rate of the peso at one U.S. dollar. Some would later joke that April 1 is Fool's Day. This system caused a rapid fall in inflation. The convertibility system required that the public finances be kept close to equilibrium in order to maintain relative prices between Argentina and the rest of the world. The government was not allowed to borrow from the Central Bank as it had done routinely over the years, but it was not prevented from borrowing from other sources including foreign sources. Domestic money (pesos) could be created only in exchange for foreign exchange. This guaranteed that the quantity of pesos in circulation would be covered by the dollars owned by the Central Bank.

The convertibility system was expected to introduce a new discipline in the public finances. Or, better, to introduce another need for equilibrium in the fiscal accounts. Never again would the public finances be so out of balance as to necessitate financing by the Central Bank. It should be pointed out that, at that time, many economists believed that fixed exchange rates, by tying the hands of policymakers, forced the latter to follow better policies. Thus, they would force the Argentine government not to run fiscal deficits that could not be easily financed by non-inflationary means. Of course, if the non-inflationary financing included foreign borrowing, this could create other difficulties, but this problem was not considered at that time. Also, when dollars were exchanged for pesos, they may also contribute to inflation.

Cavallo had invited me to visit Argentina to look at some of the economic changes that had occurred in the taxation and public finance areas and, possibly, to identify areas where further changes might be needed. He was aware that the convertibility system would survive only if the public finances were kept strictly under control. The new parity of one peso to one dollar so far had had a positive impact on the Argentine public. The fact that one could go into a shop, pay in pesos and be given change in dollars, or vice versa, at a one to one rate, was psychologically very important. The total freedom of converting pesos into dollars was a popular one. It meant a lot to most Argentines; it made them feel economically important again. It also created a constituency for stable prices and support for the Menem government. After decades of high inflation, the experience with price stability was a welcome one for most Argentines. However, the fix parity of the convertibility had not been received with much enthusiasm by the IMF and it would remain a topic of debate within the institution. This annoyed Cavallo, because he had expected a more enthusiastic support from the IMF.

In Buenos Aires, we met the relevant officials and were very impressed by the changes that had occurred in the country since August 1989. By the end of 1992, the inflation rate had fallen substantially and the fiscal accounts were close to equilibrium, if the proceeds from privatization were counted as ordinary revenue. During this period, there had been a fast process of privatization that had given a lot of revenue to the government. This was a different Argentina from the one I saw in 1989. The new Argentina seemed to have changed its attitudes, economic performance, institutions, and perhaps, what was most important, it seemed to have reacquired an optimism that was missing for a long time. A fundamental change was the attempt to scale down the role of the state through privatization and some deregulation. The changes in the tax administration had also been significant. They had been promoted by two able and determined individuals: Carlos Tacchi, who had come in as revenue secretary when Cavallo became economy minister in January 1991, and Ricardo Cosio, who had been the director of the Dirección General Impositiva (the tax administration) since the beginning of the Menem administration. They would remain in their positions until the middle of 1995, when things started to unravel.

Upon my return to Washington, I wrote a short report that was transmitted to Cavallo and to the IMF department directly responsible for following developments in Argentina, the Western Hemisphere Department, whose director at that time was Mr. Ted Beza. In this report, I recognized the many positive changes that had taken place in the country. I recognized that "the process of privatization [had] been carried further and [had] reflected more depth than anybody could have anticipated a few years [earlier]." I recognized that "the proceeds from privatization [had] contributed to the major improvement in the public finances of Argentina" and that "over the medium run, privatization should both raise tax revenue and reduce budgetary expenditures" because the privatized enterprises would no longer receive the subsidies that they had received as public enterprises and, presumably, as private enterprises they would be profitable and would pay taxes. But I also pointed out that:

"So far, however, there has not been a corresponding reduction in the size of public sector spending measured as a share of gross domestic product... Spending as a share of GDP has increased sharply over the past two years, in spite of the sharp rise in GDP, mainly because of higher transfers to provinces and higher pensions... *The improvement in the public finances has come completely from the revenue side.* Unless this improvement is accompanied by much greater controls on total public spending, the danger that the public finances may again become a major concern cannot be dismissed." In later years, the government would try to contain the cost of pensions through a pension reform that went badly and led to significant revenue losses, but it would be unable to do much about the transfers to provinces, a structural problem that had been there for a long time and would continue to be there until the present.

At the time, an aspect that worried me, which I did not include in the report for Cavallo because I had no strong evidence of it, was that in order to get higher revenue from the privatization of public enterprises, the government was making the contracts too attractive for the buyers. For example, certain monopoly powers were transferred to the private buyers when it could have been avoided, and the power of regulators was not being increased as needed. This issue, however, was out of my terms of reference so I mentioned it in some of my academic writings but not in the report to Cavallo. Of course, the buyers would be willing to pay a higher price for the enterprises to get such future benefits.

The report pointed out the good progress achieved in tax policy and in tax administration. It remarked that many of the recommendations made by the 1989 technical assistance missions had been introduced and that certain recommendations, especially those related to the broadening of the value-added tax and the use of a single rate, had produced spectacular results. Also, the changes in tax administration proposed by later missions (especially the one of creating a special unit for large taxpayers and the one punishing taxpayers who had evaded taxes by closing their place of activity for a few days) were generating good results. At the same time, the report pointed out that ". . . at least part of the improvement in tax revenue in the past two years has not resulted from the actions of the authorities but from macroeconomic factors that might not prove to be permanent. *A reversal of these factors* would have a negative impact on tax revenue."

The report listed the following factors:

1. The sharp fall in the inflation rate. Confidential estimates made by the Ministry of Economy indicated that the "Tanzi effect" had had a significant positive impact on revenue as prices fell;
2. The sharp increase in the level of imports, from about 4 billion U.S. dollars in 1990 to more than 14 billion U.S. dollars in 1992. Imports are a very important tax base for many economies and especially for developing countries. They generate a large share of the revenue from the value-added tax and other taxes. This increase in imports had contributed to higher revenue from import duties and the value-added tax;
3. The economic boom that had swollen revenue; and
4. The proceeds from privatization.

The impact of the first factor was of a "once for all" kind. The other factors would sooner or later reverse themselves. The proceeds from privatization fell significantly after 1994 because by that time most of the public enterprises had been sold.

Unfortunately, there was no reaction to this report either from the Argentine side or from the Fund's side. The attitude may have been: "the day is beautiful, the sun is shining, why worry about an eventual future storm?" The horizon of politicians, even those with Ph.D.'s in economics, is not very long and, at times, I felt that the same was true of Fund staff. There was often the inability, or simply a lack of interest, in looking beyond the short term. When I reread this report, after the Argentine default in 2001, I could not help but think of how correct its analysis was and how much foresight it contained. Unfortunately, correct forecasts, if they are for the long run, do not have the same impact as correct forecasts for the immediate future. We seem to discount the future at rates that are much too high and, thus, dismiss forecasts that predict difficulties at some distant future period.

As I tried to do often during IMF missions, I allocated some time, on weekends, to see the city and to get away from work. I felt that going from the airport to the hotel and then commuting back and forth from the hotel to government offices, sometimes for weeks, was not the best way to understand a country. Unfortunately, it often happened that time pressures combined with a lack of curiosity made many Fund missions learn about a country mainly from the numbers that were fed to them by the nation's authorities. I recall Michel Camdessus, the IMF's managing director at the time, urging Fund missions to spend some time trying to see and understand the countries they visited. But few did, perhaps because of the work ethic of the institution. As it used to be said about French bikinis, the numbers that the missions collected often revealed a lot but managed to hide the essentials. Through these numbers, a country became a set of statistics and little else. In this 1992 mission, Partho Shome and I spent a few hours over the weekend sightseeing and engaging in some cultural activities before returning to Washington.

Given my interest in paintings, especially in naïf paintings, we visited a private gallery called Galería Zurbarán. Its owner, Ignacio, a very charming and knowledgeable individual, had met the IMF's managing director, whose daughter was a talented artist, and he was very nice to us. Ignacio was a real encyclopedia on Argentine art and gave each of us a large book that he had written on that art. He also showed us some marvelous Argentine paintings. Unfortunately, he did not have any of the naïf paintings that I collected so I was not tempted by what he showed us. The high prices discouraged me as well. Luckily, there was at that time a good exhibition of Argentine naïfs at Patio Bullrich. Some of them were very good and still affordable and I bought three paintings, two by an artist called Teresa Carabassa, and one by Alicia Messing. One of the Carabassa paintings depicted a tango scene while the other one represented the joy, in an obviously prosperous family, of the recent birth of a child. That painting was titled "Nació Benjamin." The proud mother is shown holding the child in a large and beautiful room full of paintings and antique furniture while the family is toasting with champagne. The accent on antiques, paintings and culture makes the scene very "old Europe." It was another manifestation of the cultural links Argentina had with the Europe of a century ago. The other painting shows two maids wearing neat and identical uniforms, each holding one of two twins. The title of this painting was "Gemelos." Once again, the cultural and European influence is unmistakable.

At the exhibition, there were two other paintings by the same artists that I thought were really very good. One represented another, but better, tango scene with many dancers; the other one called *Va a llover* (it is going to rain) contained a nun riding a zebra in a forest. The nun was shown in the act of opening an umbrella. It was a truly charming naïf. I was disappointed to find out that both paintings had already been sold. Women seem to be the majority among naïf painters. Naïf painters are common in many Latin American countries; although in none of these countries have their paintings become such a significant export as in Haiti. But major individual painters have come out of countries such as Ecuador (Endara Crow), Honduras (José Antonio Velásquez), etc.

Inspired by the exhibition at Patio Bullrich, we visited La Boca, the famous area around the port of Buenos Aires. La Boca was the quarter where especially Italian immigrants settled after arriving from Europe, in the early part of the last century. It was crowded especially by Genoese sailors and dock workers. They may have influenced the accent of the Argentines living in that area. La Boca is largely the place where tango flourished. Now La Boca is a touristy place full of typical restaurants and nightclubs but, in the past, it was a rough neighborhood teeming with brothels and cheap places to eat. It is picturesque because of the lively and strong colors of many of its buildings. La Boca was the place where boats and ships came for repairs and for occasional repainting. Often, there was some paint left over and that's where the strong colors—yellow, green, and red—came from. This leftover paint was used to color the houses and buildings in the area and has made La Boca an attractive place for naïf or primitive painters.

One of these painters, who became especially famous in Argentina, was Benito Quinquela Martín. He was the illegitimate child of a woman from a prominent, old, and traditional family. His birth was an embarrassment for the family so he was kept away from it. He became one of Argentina's best known painters—he painted mostly scenes from La Boca—and his paintings have a primitive and unmistakable look. Now there is a nice museum named after him in the area of La Boca, which we visited and highly recommend, especially to those who want to have a feel for the area and the atmosphere that must have characterized Buenos Aires in the early part of the last century.

We also walked to Caminito, the famous small street that is no longer than, perhaps, 100 meters (300 feet). Flanking Caminito are the typical houses painted by Quinquela Martín and a few benches where one can sit and rest for a while. It is a colorful alley where some artists try to sell their work and musicians enliven the atmosphere with their music. There is nothing that would make this little street famous except for the fact that one of the best known tangos, *Caminito*, has the same name. Given the importance of tango in Argentina, Caminito has become a tourist attraction. Of course, wherever there are tourists in Buenos Aires one can find tango bands and, occasionally, tango dancers. An interesting characteristic of the couples who dance tango in the streets is that the men are often elderly gentlemen who, in look and behavior seem to come straight from a century ago, while the women are often voluptuous and attractive young women. I could never understand why this age contrast is so common among tango dancers. In the bands, the *bandoneón* is now the most typical instrument. It is the instrument that makes a band a "tango band" even though, apparently, it was introduced decades after tango was born. It came from Germany and is supposed to be quite difficult to play.

Given my interest in photography, I carried my camera during the visit to La Boca and Caminito and took a few pictures. One of these pictures is of a sad and lonely-looking man and an elderly woman who are seating near each other but on two different benches. In spite of their relative proximity, they seem to be totally unaware of, or indifferent to, each other's presence. The clean stump of a tree cuts the photo into two distinct areas adding to the sense of separation. When I returned to Washington, I had the photo developed and entered it, with the title "Solitude," into the Annual Photographic Exhibition, organized jointly by the World Bank and the IMF. This is a large exhibition with many formidable competitors. To my surprise and delight, the photo won the first prize. In Caminito, there was another elderly lady trying to sell naïf paintings, mostly nativity scenes as it was shortly before Christmas. They were not particularly good but, after chatting with her and being told that she had not sold a single painting all day, I bought one more as an act of charity than as an investment in art. But, for some reason, the painting has taken a place in my house not justified by its artistic merit.

Quinquela Martín made me think about the market prices of paintings. I have noted that the prices are often affected by a kind of "preferred habitat" effect. Some painters acquire a local reputation that does not carry outside their areas or countries. In part, but only in part, this is due to lack of information. Sentimental or even chauvinistic reasons contribute to it. This means that, at times, the local prices tend to be much higher than the values they would have in other areas or countries, even if there were full information. This, in a way, provides a kind of rent to the painters or, more often, to those who own these paintings. I observed direct evidence of this phenomenon once at an auction house in Washington, D.C. A painting by an Austrian artist had been put up for auction. The expected price was listed in the catalogue at $6,000. However, when the bidding started there were a few people bidding from Austria over the phone. To the surprise of everyone in the room, the painting was finally sold to an Austrian bidder for $150,000. Obviously, the painter was far more famous or more desired in his own country than in the international market. This means that when the economy of a large country, say Russia or China, starts doing well, the works of art of that country begin to be demanded by the rich in that country. Russian paintings that have recently come up for sale at major auction houses have seen their prices go up sharply because of the demand by rich Russian oligarchs. The same is happening with Chinese art objects.

One last place we visited was San Telmo, an old area of Buenos Aires where there are now numerous restaurants and antique shops and where, on Sundays, there is a colorful outdoor antique market. The market takes place in a plaza that fills to capacity with sellers, shoppers and window shoppers. The plaza becomes like the stage of a big show because, in addition to antiques, there are the inevitable scenes of tango dancers. Some are very good and colorful. I recall an interesting couple: the male was an old gentleman with a long white beard that made him resemble Giuseppe Garibaldi, the hero of the Italian Risorgimento; while the woman was young and curvaceous, with the strong legs that characterize tango dancers. Their dancing was very graceful and elegant and they attracted a large crowd of admirers. They seemed to enjoy being at the center of attraction and did not look at all embarrassed. Their faces glowed with pride.

Over the years, I became a tango aficionado and saw many shows. I came to feel that, when it is danced well, this is the most sensuous and beautiful dance in the world. The beginning of tango has been traced to sometime between 1880 and 1890 in Buenos Aires. It started as a popular expression of the lower class and was initially danced in brothels and other places frequented by young and poor workers, who were often freshly arrived immigrants. Over the following century, it became a world phenomenon danced in France, Russia, Japan, Italy, and many other places. While there's no doubt about its time and place of origin, there is a lot of uncertainty about the origin of the term "tango." At least 22 possibilities have been mentioned, but it is likely that the term came from Africa and the tango originated from African music that, over the years, went through a process of transformation and even globalization mixing with other music, some from southern Italy, to produce a totally different product (See Andrés Carreteros's *El Tango, la Otra Historia* [Buenos Aires: Ediciones Margus, 2004]). The combination of music, songs, and dance makes tango an especially attractive form of art. Carlos Gardel is considered the most famous tango singer of all times. Tango combines passion, tenderness, romance, sadness, betrayal, despair, and melancholy as no other form of music does with the possible exception of Portuguese fado. A common joke is that tango is especially popular in Chile because in many tango songs someone (obviously an Argentine) dies. It is a well known fact that Chileans are not particularly fond of Argentines.

At the time when tango was born, Argentina was receiving a lot of immigrants from Europe, especially from southern Europe, with a large majority of Italians. In 1914–1930, 30 percent of the Argentine population was born abroad with 80 percent of the immigrants being Italians or Spaniards. Many were poor immigrants from Italian rural areas. These immigrants were so humble and unsophisticated that the Italian Embassy in Buenos Aires felt it necessary to distribute to new Italian immigrants a list of instructions on how to behave in the new urban setting. These instructions included tips on how to address people, how to order food, and so on. The list is now displayed in the Museum of Immigrants in Buenos Aires.

At that time, two Argentine leaders, Domingo F. Sarmiento and Juan Bautista Alberdi, debated on what kind of immigrants should be allowed into Argentina. The debate was reminiscent of current debates in Europe and the United States. Sarmiento wanted immigrants with human capital and not the poor, largely illiterate immigrants coming from Italy, Spain and other Southern or Eastern European countries. Alberdi argued that these immigrants would produce children that would have human capital. In fact, an obsession for many of these poor and illiterate immigrants was to have a child that would complete higher education. A famous theater play called *Mi hijo el doctor* (my son, the doctor), abbreviated into "Mijo el dotor," typified this attitude. Of course, here the title "doctor" did not refer to medical doctors but to individuals with a higher education. Italians contributed significantly to the development of tango. In fact, many of the major Tango players or composers were of Italian background. Astor Piazzolla, Osvaldo Pugliese, Omero Manzi, Lucio de Mare, Alfredo de Angelis, Pedro Mafia, and others would distinguish themselves as tango composers or tango players, thus contributing to the italianization of tango.

The immigrants fell largely into four groups: the "tanos" were the Italians; the "gallegos" were those from Spain; the "rusos" were mostly the Jews from Eastern European countries and Russia; and the "turcos" where all those from the Ottoman Empire, including Arabs and Turks. A law passed in 1884 (law 1420) had provided free education for Argentina's inhabitants and made attendance to elementary school obligatory. This contributed to the growth of the Argentine economy. A law passed in 1904 had made military service obligatory, while another law passed in 1914 had made voting obligatory. These laws contributed to making the children of immigrants feel Argentine quickly. Education had the double purpose of making children "literate" and "patriotic," creating a strong sense of nationalism. There were also early laws that provided pensions to public employees. Argentina was obviously well ahead of much of the world in social legislation. By the beginning of the twentieth century, Argentina had a higher literacy rate than many European countries and had become a sophisticated and cosmopolitan country with strong cultural and commercial links to Europe.

In October 1994, I was invited back to Buenos Aires by Mr. Marcos Victorica, the president of the Instituto de Estudios Contemporáneos (IEC) at the time, to be part of an honor committee that would present a special citation to Carlos Tacchi, the revenue secretary. This prize was given annually to the person who, in the judgment of the IEC, had contributed most significantly to the success of the Argentine economy in that year. President Menem had received the prize in 1991 and Domingo Cavallo in 1992. The chairman of the honor committee in 1994 was President Menem and I was the only foreign member. I felt very honored by this invitation because I was told that, in the two previous years, the invited foreign members had been Henry Kissinger and David Rockefeller respectively. I was also very pleased because of the admiration I had developed for Carlos Tacchi.

The year 1994 was, in many ways, the best year for Argentina in a very long time. The economy had been growing for five consecutive years at the fastest rate in Latin America. In the 1990–1994 period, the growth rate had averaged a spectacular 7.9 percent per year, while the inflation rate had fallen to only about 4 percent per year from the 5000 percent rate reached in 1989. Argentina had risen to the rank of a "tiger" in economic performance. Considering that in the 1960–2002 period Argentina had suffered seventeen years of negative growth rates and that the 1975–1990 period would be defined as one of deep depression, it is easy to see how extraordinary this performance was considered both nationally and internationally. The share of taxes into GDP, including social security contributions, had reached 22 percent *of the much higher GDP*, having risen by 6 percent of GDP since 1989. So, having seen its real income grow phenomenally, the government had a lot of money that it could spend. This increase was in part due to the efforts of Carlos Tacchi, who was being honored that evening. He had taken over his job with a dedication and a determination that acquired him the reputation of being a kind of Taliban of taxation; or a true fundamentalist of taxation. In spite of this success, however, Argentina continued to have a fiscal deficit for the public sector close to 2 percent of GDP. This should have made some alarms go off both in Washington and in Buenos Aires.

In 1994 there was a lot of euphoria in Buenos Aires. It seemed that Argentina had finally regained its place in the sun and God was Argentine again. The country had become the darling of the international financial community and the celebration to honor Tacchi was one way in which the Argentine society would commemorate the country's success. I arrived in Buenos Aires accompanied by my wife on the morning of October 26, in the middle of the Argentine spring. It was a splendid sunny day. We stayed at the Caesar Park Hotel, in front of Patio Bullrich, where they used to auction cattle but which now is one of Buenos Aires' most elegant shopping malls. The reception for Tacchi would take place that evening in the same hotel and it would involve the cream of the Argentine society.

In the evening, the huge ballroom of the hotel started filling with elegant ladies and gentlemen. We met Carlos Tacchi and his charming wife, Anita, who had been a valuable accomplice in his fight to reduce tax evasion. She was used by Carlos to check whether shops were giving receipts for their sales. These receipts facilitated the collection of the value-added tax. The beginning of the ceremony itself was delayed by the late arrival of President Menem. When Menem arrived, Tacchi took me to greet him and the president said that he remembered me from our meeting in September 1989.

I had been asked to give the "laudatio" for Carlos Tacchi. I gave a short speech, in Spanish, paying compliments to his personality, his integrity, and his work as the revenue secretary. I complimented him and the Argentine authorities for the success they had achieved in reducing tax evasion and in increasing the tax ratio. I elaborated on the role that Carlos Tacchi, and his wife, had played in that success. And I added that the government should make an equivalent effort at reducing public spending, which remained too high. I stressed that the fiscal imbalance that still existed could not, and should not, be corrected only from the revenue side.

The speech seemed to hit the right tone. At the end of the ceremony, I received compliments from many people and, especially, from Tacchi's relatives. Some even complimented my Spanish, which I was told had a pleasant Italian intonation. President Menem spoke at the end and graciously mentioned the "Tacchi effect" and the "Tanzi effect" as the two forces that had led to the increase in tax revenue. As usual, he was charming and charismatic. His speech was followed by a reception where I had the opportunity to meet some of Argentina's successful industrialists. In these meetings I sensed that the prevailing feeling was that Argentina had finally found the right way and was returning to its rightful place among developed countries.

The next day, I had some meetings to discuss areas in which the Fund had been of assistance to Argentina in making institutional reforms. I met Ricardo Cosio, at the tax administration, and Ricardo Gutiérrez, who was then in charge of the budget. From him I got a demonstration of progress toward the establishment of a treasury system with a single account (cuenta única). This single account would replace some 3,000–4,000 existing separate accounts, which would make it possible to determine the status of the fiscal statistics on a cash basis quickly and currently. The pursuit of good fiscal policy is, of course, much easier when the relevant information on the current situation is available rapidly, and that information is comprehensive rather than limited to only parts of public spending. A single account is obviously just a useful instrument; by itself it does not guarantee that good policy will be pursued. But it can be useful. This was one of several institutional reforms that Cavallo was trying to enact at that time. Gutiérrez had received help from various sources, including the IMF, for this reform. We had assisted him by sending Pedro Parente, our expert from Brazil, who would later become minister in the Henrique Cardozo administration. Parente was an expert on the organization of treasuries. Gutierrez mentioned to me that he thought that the system that existed in Spain was the best. He was proud of the progress made.

I was interviewed by *Clarín*, a leading Argentine newspaper, on the progress on tax reform in Argentina. I answered that there had been progress. "Do the results conform with the proposals of the Tanzi mission in 1989?" "Yes, broadly." "Is a VAT rate of 18 percent too high?" "It is on the high side, but not exceptionally. There are other countries with even higher rates." In later years, against my advice, the VAT rate would be raised to 21 percent. "Is it fair to tax only or mostly consumption?" "It depends on how tax revenue is used." "What about strengthening the income tax?" "Yes, if more revenue is needed and the possibilities with the VAT have been exhausted." At that time, tax revenue was sharply up especially if measured in real terms and not as a share of GDP. It was up for the reasons I have described earlier, including macroeconomic developments such as the fast rates of growth and the collapse of inflation, in addition to the work that Tacchi and Cosio were doing in implementing the 1989 tax reform.

Administrative improvements had been so impressive under the guidance of Tacchi and Cosio that a delegation was sent from China to study them. Some of these improvements had to do with the widespread withholding system on payments made to the suppliers, which Tacchi had introduced, and with the reorganization of the tax administration on the advice of the Fiscal Affairs Department of the IMF. One proposal had been to create a "Large Taxpayers Unit" for the top taxpayers in the country and to develop the best techniques available for controlling them. These taxpayers paid an overwhelming proportion of all tax revenue. The strategy was that once these taxpayers were well controlled, the techniques and methods developed for them would be applied progressively to larger and larger groups until the administration for all taxpayers improved. This technique, at least in its earlier phase, had proven successful. The problem was that it required a sustained effort over long periods of time and this effort would not be maintained in later years.

When I visited Domingo Cavallo, who by now had been the minister of economy for almost four years, I found him in a very good mood. He was charming and friendly. We discussed the current economic situation, which was very good, and the problem with high pensions which was a bit worrisome. Pensions absorbed a large share of spending and were growing fast. Cavallo told me that a reform that would establish funded individual accounts was being planned. The IMF had not been asked to assist with this reform. At this time, Cavallo was popular with entrepreneurs but was seen as too aggressive and too rigid or abrasive. The impression that I got was that he was respected but not loved, but then again I would have worried about a finance minister loved by industrialists. Nevertheless, I could not help asking myself whether he would have a political future. Rumors had started to circulate that he would like to become president of Argentina after Menem, and this might have created some tension between them. During this social visit, Cavallo told me about the Perito Moreno glacier in Los Glaciares National Park in southern Patagonia; he described it as the eighth wonder of the world. I had not heard about this place and thought that Cavallo's description of it was a typical Argentine exaggeration. Nevertheless, he convinced me that we should visit it. Before I could say no, he had already requested one of his assistants to organize the trip.

That night, my wife and I were invited by Carlos Tacchi to a big formal dinner at the Sheraton Hotel organized by "Conciencia," an association of successful women and wives of successful men. It was a large and elegant affair organized to raise money for charitable work. Many of the entrepreneurs' wives were beautiful and stylish I met several successful entrepreneurs who had been born in Italy or descended from Italian immigrants. They seemed genuinely happy to meet me. Some carried distinguished Italian last names (Einaudi, Martini), which were household names in Argentina, indicating how close the two countries had been over the years. The dinner was attended by President Menem who, together with Mr. Bullrich, a man from one of Argentina's old and prominent families, led the auction of a new car. There was a lot of bidding and the spirit of altruism, or the desire to impress those present, pushed the bidding for the car to a very high level. At the end, Menem gave a speech in which he referred to his current life as "walking on a bed of roses that still had some thorns." In this period, he had started having serious problems with his wife so it was not clear whether the thorns were in his personal or presidential life. Officially, this must have been the best period of his political career, but it was a period that would soon come to an end.

CHAPTER VII

It Wasn't All Fiscal: A Visit to Patagonia

At the end of October 1994, my wife and I flew from Buenos Aires to Río Gallegos, a town of about 70,000 inhabitants in the province of Santa Cruz in Patagonia. We took on a full, three-hour flight straight south. I had always thought of Buenos Aires (or Santiago in Chile) as more or less the end of the American continent, but I had to get used to the idea that one could fly straight south from Buenos Aires for hours and still be on the continent. Patagonia is a huge area, the size of France and Spain combined. It is a very diverse and sparsely populated area.

When we arrived in Río Gallegos, we were met by our guide Gabriela and Gustavo, our driver. They would be with us for the whole tour. After collecting our luggage, we left for our hotel. The hotel was loacted in a small town called Calafate after a Patagonian flower. Gabriella informed us that the hotel was 350 km, about 200 miles, away! That is close to the Washington, D.C.–New York distance, about a four-hour drive. The road from Río Gallegos to Calafate is mostly tundra. During much of the year, it is too windy and too cold for anything but the smallest plants and shrubs to grow. There are no trees, no houses, no signs of any human activity—nothing on the way. However, about half way to Calafate, say about 200 km from Río Gallegos and from anywhere, there was finally a sign of life: a very small settlement (ten people) with a couple of buildings that accommodated a gasoline station, a health station, and a small diner. The place was appropriately called La Esperanza (Hope).

We stopped at La Esperanza to refuel, have something to eat, and use the restrooms. Obviously, the available food was steak. The lady who served us was remarkably sophisticated for a place like this. This was a constant Argentine characteristic, one found very sophisticated people in the most unusual places. She told us that one would be imprudent to be caught without gas on the road because this was one of the windiest places on earth and, in the winter, the temperature could plunge to −30 degrees Celsius or even lower. After our rest, we drove through this desolate area toward Calafate. We rarely saw another car, or any people or houses by the road. I wondered what one would do in case the car broke down, especially in winter. Fortunately, the road was in reasonably good condition and the car could move at good speed. The driver seemed to know where there were potholes so he could slow down when he needed to. After about four hours driving, we finally got to Calafate and were taken to Posada Los Alamos, the lodge where we had reservations. Calafate is a small town which, in 1994, had about 3,000 inhabitants. It seemed to be literally at the end of the world. I found it strange to be in a town without traffic lights, pollution, dirt, traffic jams, or noise, and with apparently no crime. The problems of the world seemed to be far away but they might get closer after the construction of an airport was completed within a few years. The airport would make the trip to Perito Moreno much easier for tourists, but perhaps less interesting.

During the flight to Río Gallegos and the long ride to Calafate, I felt a bit sick. The fried squid I had eaten the night before at a restaurant in Buenos Aires had probably not agreed with my stomach. The night of our arrival I felt tired, so we decided to go to bed early and I soon fell asleep profoundly. Around 2:00 a.m., I heard someone opening the door to our room and I woke up. I asked who was there and heard someone mumble an apology and close the door. As a precaution, I placed a piece of furniture behind the door and, the next morning, reported the incident to the hotel's front desk. They promised to investigate. The next day, the culprit came to apologize—he was one of the hotel's guests and had simply gone to the wrong room. Probably all the rooms had identical locks and keys.

The morning after our arrival the car picked us up to take us to the Perito Moreno glacier, the main destination of our trip. It would be another 100 km going west to get there but, unlike the road from Río Gallegos, this was a very interesting road. Because the mountains provide some protection from the high winds, the vegetation was more diverse and there were even some trees along the road. The whole area is made up of huge land holdings (estancias), some as large as small countries. These estancias can raise mainly sheep because of the harsh weather and the extremely low fertility of the land. I was told that it takes anywhere between 1 and 4 acres to sustain a single sheep, and that the ratio between acreage needed and sheep sustained has been rising over the years because the sheep's grazing has been progressively eroding the land. Only huge estancias can survive because of the low fertility of the land and (at that time) the low price of wool.

Some of these estancias are so huge that they need to have a few small cottages spread miles apart to provide shelter for the gauchos (the farm workers or sheep boys) who, with the help a few sheep dogs, control and gather the sheep when necessary. The sheep are free to wander as they please within these huge fenced areas. They live permanently outside and are collected and sheared in the spring so that, by the next winter, they have the protection of new wool. Winters are very hard for them because, in addition to the cold, they have difficulty finding food as snow covers the little grass and the small shrubs that feed them. Some do not make it and, when they die, they are left abandoned and become food for scavengers, of which there are many.

Gauchos are special people. They have become part of the Argentine folklore, just like cowboys have become part of the American folklore. Some tango songs are dedicated to them and to their life. They live alone and hardly see, or talk with, anyone. For the most part, they never marry. They spend their days on the back of their horses and wear the "facón," a special knife they use for eating (normally meat), for occasionally skinning sheep, and, when necessary, for self-defense.

On the road to Perito Moreno glacier, we visited a place where they shear sheep. We also saw some sheep dogs in action. One literally held up our car by standing in the middle of the road. It prevented the car from moving forward while hundreds of sheep crossed the road in front of us. I had never thought that a dog could perform so efficiently the job of a traffic cop. The moment the last sheep had crossed, the dog moved letting our car go forward. It was a truly impressive performance.

We visited an estancia where a small seven-room hotel called Hostería Alta Vista had recently been built. It had been built in the hope that tourism would increase, which seemed very likely at that time given the growth performance and the increasing popularity of Argentina. This was a time when many rich Americans were buying some of these estancias in Patagonia. The manager ("gerente") was Verónica Ayling De Miglioli. The hotel was absolutely charming. Everything was spotless and in good taste. It reminded me of the quaint small country hotels that one can find in certain parts of France and Italy. It would be a great place to spend a few days, literally away from the world; miles away from everything, including bad news. Unfortunately, it was the end of October and no guests had yet arrived. The hotel had opened in the mid-September and would remain open for only six months. Unfortunately for the hotel, not too many people came to the end of the world.

The road to Perito Moreno glacier is splendid. We saw numerous breathtaking sights, lots of sheep, a few cows, and many wild rabbits, horses and birds. The cows and horses lived mainly in areas protected from the winds by the mountains. We saw eagles, condors, and other vultures. These birds of prey have an easy life because of the many sheep that die and are left abandoned. We saw some of these dead sheep. These vultures (or "caroñeros") would have an occasional real feast when pumas descended on the sheep accompanied by younger pumas. To teach the younger pumas how to kill, the pumas might kill as many as 20, 30 or even more sheep at a time, leaving a lot of food for the vultures to feast on. We did not see any pumas, who apparently sleep during the day, but were assured that they were there. But we did see some animals (guanacos) belonging to the family of the llamas. The colors of the sky and the shape of the clouds were unique. They gave a strange Patagonian mood to the sights.

The Perito Moreno glacier is just one of the 200 glaciers that form part of Los Glaciares National Park, but it is the best known. The national park covers an area of some 14,000 square kilometers. Perito Moreno covers over 200 of them. In recent decades, it has been advancing into Lake Argentino. Every few years, it advances to the point where it cuts the long lake in two parts. When this happens, the water levels on both sides of the lake become different. Thus the glacier becomes a kind of natural dam that holds the water from the side where the level is higher and keeps becoming progressively higher. Over time, tremendous pressure builds on the glacier until, at some point, the dam breaks and the water from the higher level empties into the lower level with tremendous force and thunderous noise. It is reported to be one of the world's great spectacles. It happened while we were there and was photographed by a Japanese team that had waited weeks to catch the event. It would happen again on March 15, 2004, fifteen years after that time.

I had never seen anything more striking than Perito Moreno. The view of the two sides of the lake, with the glacier thrusting in and surrounded by huge snow-covered mountains, is unparalleled. The color of the glacier is the most beautiful blue. From the well-designed wooden observatory platform (which has different levels), one can see the details of the glacier with all its crevasses and, frequently, huge pieces of ice detaching and falling into the lake with big roars.

We spent a few hours staring at the glacier and I indulged in one of my passions—photography. I was hoping to win another prize! We had lunch, a steak sandwich, at a small restaurant not far from the observatory.

Gabriela, our guide, was born in Buenos Aires but liked her life in Calafate. She said that she worked six months, the tourist season which took place from October to March, and then relaxed for the next six months. Her only worry was having enough money until the following season. She said that there is nothing to do in Calafate in winter—there are no movie houses, no libraries, no bars, and only one or two restaurants remain open. This gives families an opportunity to spend a lot of time together inside. In winter it is too cold and windy to do anything outside. I hoped that the family members did not develop cases of cabin fever!

Gustavo, our driver, was from Córdoba. He was also very nice. It turned out that the lady who had served our breakfast that morning at Posada Los Alamos was his wife and was expecting a child. His wife's father had died the past February in a fire because the firemen had not had a truck to reach the house in time. Now, they had a truck but did not have a place to store it. The truck had been kept outside since May. It had cost as much as $300,000.

On the morning of our departure from Calafate, there was no water or electricity at the hotel and they had not come back by the time we left. As a result, we could not take a shower and I could not shave. We drove, with Gustavo, the 350 km back to Río Gallegos. We stopped again at La Esperanza and had a good lunch. We spoke with the owner, another fairly sophisticated lady, who commented on the isolation of the place—no telephones—especially in winter. Water and electricity were generated locally. Supplies came once a week (in the good season) from Río Gallegos. The people who worked at La Esperanza, mostly young men, got two days off every two weeks to visit their families in Calafate or Río Gallegos. No children lived in La Esperanza.

During the second lap of the trip (La Esperanza to Río Gallegos), the weather deteriorated. We saw a strange sight: thousands of sheep moving in one direction in a single line. It was the first time I had seen such a large number of sheep together and the first time I had seen any order among sheep. Apparently, instinct makes the sheep follow (in single file) a leader that takes them to an area that offers some protection from the inclement weather. This must be the origin of the famous "herd instinct" expression that we hear so much in financial markets. It was interesting for me to see where the expression comes from and I wondered how the sheep pick their leader. They obviously do not hold elections! What instinctive or explicit process leads to the choice? Do they make mistakes? Is the leader always the same sheep? Does it insist that they "stay the course"? I had no answers for these questions.

A footnote on the gauchos: Gustavo told us that when they receive their monthly wage (about $200 at that time), many of them go to town and some spend all of it in one night drinking or gambling (there is a casino in Calafate!). He did not mention women but I assumed that they were also a part of the spending spree. Gauchos are considered very unusual, solitary, and eccentric types! On the way to Río Gallegos, we also saw a group of about 50 horses. One of them had a bell around the neck. The others followed this horse (yegua madrina), which was obviously the leader. This is a different kind of "herd instinct" because there is a mechanical signal that provides specific instructions and identifies the leader so, perhaps, it should not be considered "herd instinct."

When we reached Río Gallegos, we were surprised to see a Boeing 747. It was strange to see such a huge plane in such a small and isolated place. The plane was on the way to Australia (Aerolíneas Argentinas airline). It had stopped at Río Gallegos for refueling for the long flight. This flight was discontinued in later years when Aerolíneas Argentinas went through financial difficulties.

We arrived in Buenos Aires at 9:00 p.m. It was cold and raining hard. We were taken to Caesar Park, where Carlos Tacchi and his wife, Anita, had been waiting for a long time. They were elegantly dressed and I was wearing casual clothes and had not shaved since the morning of the previous day. My wife did not have the problem of shaving but she had not been able to change either. Without dressing up, we left for a marvelous, elegant restaurant (Happening in La Recoleta) and had the best meat we had ever had. As usual, the Tacchis were very warm and charming.

The next morning, I gave a not so great lecture on taxation and globalization at San Andrés University, one of the successful private universities that have sprung up in Latin America. These universities have shown that in many subjects, such as economics, finance, business administration, law, computer sciences and others, the private sector can do a good job in replacing the services provided by the public sector. In my lecture, I talked too much and could not make my talk as interesting and analytical as I would have liked, in spite of the fact that I had just finished writing a book on the subject for the Brookings Institution and was considered an expert on it. I had been invited to give the lecture by Osvaldo Schenone, an Argentine economist who had worked occasionally as a consultant for the Fiscal Affairs Department of the IMF. After the lecture, my wife and I went straight to the domestic airport for a trip to Trelew, from where we would visit Península de Valdés, located on the east coast of Patagonia, south of Buenos Aires. This is the northern part of Patagonia and it is less cold. At the airport, I ran into Governor Angeloz (the governor of Córdoba) and former presidential candidate, whom I had met a few years earlier at a North–South Conference in Portugal organized by Animal Cavaco Silva, Portugal's prime minister at the time. He recognized me and greeted me warmly. The "Tanzi effect" still carried some value even though prices had stabilized in Argentina and nobody talked about it any more.

Upon arrival in Trelew, we were met by a guide and our driver, Mr. Protti, and started our extremely interesting excursion of this part of Patagonia, in the province of Chubut. Our guide, Rubén Mariezcurrena, was an encyclopedia on Patagonia. He told us that the name Patagonia meant "big feet." Apparently, the first people seen by Magellan (Magallanes) when he reached this part of the world were very tall indigenous people with unusually big feet. On the way to the hotel where we would be staying, we visited a charming little town (Gaimán) inhabited mostly by descendents of 19th-century Welsh immigrants. A tea house, Ty Nayer (Museo del Té), could have come straight out of 19th-century Wales. All the furniture was authentic and charming. It is interesting how some national groups have managed to preserve their national identity and their traditions in the New World. One has the impression of going back in time to different places. We visited two protestant churches and, afterward, stopped by a fishing port, Puerto Rawson, at the time of the day when fishing boats were coming back full of fish. The amount of fish they carried would have made the fishermen in the Italian town where I was born very envious. Sea lions and lots of birds were wandering around. Both were waiting for discarded fish. The fishermen were friendly and the fish very cheap in a country that consumes more meat per capita than any other country in the world (about 70 kilos per year).

Our hotel, La Rosada de Madryn, was right by the sea in Puerto Madryn. Our room had a beautiful ocean view. Puerto Madryn is a small town by a large gulf where whales come to mate during the summer making this even a significant tourist attraction. On the first night we dined at an inexpensive but exceptionally good restaurant near the hotel called Mi Pequeño Restaurant. We ate some of the best fish we had ever had!

The next morning at 8:00 a.m. we met Gustavo Díaz, the owner of the catamaran *Gandul*. He told us that he had crossed the Atlantic two years earlier with this relatively small but comfortable boat, accompanied by his wife, their two small children, and a couple of companion sailors. He had gone to Sevilla, Spain, to attend the 500th anniversary of the discovery of America. He had designed and built the boat himself and was obviously very proud of it. "Gandul," which means lazy, was a name given to him by his father-in-law, who did not approve of the fact that he did not have a steady job. Gustavo was a handsome, pleasant, and enthusiastic fellow with an adventurous spirit and a contagious laugh. He told us that he was planning to go around the world in his catamaran with his family.

To get to the *Gandul* we had to descend a steep ladder at the pier, get in a plastic "gomón" (a kind of small life rubber boat) and climb into the catamaran. Because there was almost no wind, Gustavo had to use the small engine of the catamaran in order to move. Normally, the boat was moved by the pressure of the wind on its sails. Since our objective was to see the whales that crowd the bay in front of Puerto Madryn, he did not like to use the engine as it disturbs them. Slowly, our boat got to an area where we began to see a few whales in the distance. We admired their gigantic bodies swimming graciously through the water, we listened to their beautiful but strange noises, and we followed their playful body movements. Their jumps out of the water were terrific sights and made loud sounds. I tried to take some photos of them but was disappointed—they kept their distance from the boat (a couple of hundred meters). Our attempts to get closer were not immediately successful, perhaps because the engine had disturbed them. We saw penguins and sea lions swimming in the water and lots and lots of birds. Some of these birds were fishing and having an easy time at that.

We had been there for a while waiting for the whales to get closer when, suddenly, clouds covered the sky and it started raining (I seem to bring rain to the places I visit). Soon, the rain was accompanied by winds that became progressively stronger, and before we knew it, we were in the middle of a real storm. The sea, calm up to now, started moving and increasingly larger waves formed. Mr. Protti, our driver, and Madeleine, my first wife, started feeling sick. Protti was obviously scared. Gustavo and the other members of the crew made preparations to go back, but the direction of the wind—coming from exactly the direction where we wanted to go—made it difficult. The boat was jumping quite a bit and the waves were making us wet. I tried to keep calm thinking that this same boat had crossed the Atlantic so it should be safe within a gulf, but I could not help but worry. Gustavo decided to lead the boat toward an area, a few miles from the pier, where it would benefit from the different direction of the wind and the protection offered by some hills. After a suspenseful period that seemed an eternity, we came close to the beach. Since it was protected by high hills, the sea was much calmer there. We were transferred to the rubber boat, two at a time, and taken to shore (just next to a sunken ship!). We were happy to be on firm ground again.

In the afternoon, we went to an area that reminded me of Dante's *Inferno*. It was a natural park well above sea level with an observatory that looked down to the sea and into a huge cavern. Inside were thousands of sea lions, which had separated themselves in groups made up of a male (the fighter), several females, and their offspring. The males could be identified by their much larger size. They established territorial rights and would fight with other lions to keep them away from their territory (a small piece of the beach) and from their females. The problem was that, at the time we were there, the high tides were coming in, thus progressively reducing the size of the land and pushing the whole group into an increasingly smaller area. Lots of fights erupted with horrible sounding cries. Some of the lions were trying to move by literally walking on top of others. It was a horrific and scary scene that somehow reminded me of the fighting in Bosnia at that time, and of other human problems where hundreds of people find themselves crowded in small spaces. In his book *Collapse*, Jared Diamond explained the tragedy in Rwanda in similar terms.

The next morning, we left the hotel at 8:30 to visit Isla de los Pájaros (the island of the birds). Antoine de St. Exupéry, the famous French writer of *The Little Prince*, spent three months in this area. We were told that the shape of the island is reflected in *The Little Prince*, in the drawing, of a snake eating an elephant. The island is off-limits but it can be observed through powerful binoculars. It is packed with a huge number of birds of all kinds. More birds than can be seen anywhere else.

Our next destination was Península de Valdés. Here, the distances are huge and the place is practically empty. Because of the salinity of the land, which had been submerged in the ocean for millions of years, only wild grass and shrubs grow. It is strange to see hundreds of kilometers without trees. In Península de Valdés, we stopped at a beach to see sea elephants, mammals that I had never seen before and I did not even know existed. We stopped at a place where our guide's uncle had a little stand where one could get coffee. We chatted with the man and his wife. They were ranchers with low incomes who owned a lot of land. In that part of the world, that is not a contradiction. All ranchers there owned vast amounts of land because the only thing the land supports is sheep and one needs 2–3 hectares per sheep. The time of our arrival coincided with a solar eclipse, which gave a strange look to an already strange place. The whole mood was extra-terrestrial. From the back of the stand we descended toward the beach. Because of the eclipse, it had gotten dark; it was also foggy, windy, and cold. It was a truly strange and spooky place.

We walked down to the beach through a path that had been created for visitors. As we descended, about 50 meters, we began to see some strange, huge creatures. They were the sea elephants, or gigantic seals, which can weigh thousands of kilos. I had never seen them and was surprised by their size and look. There was a large number of them—males, females and several young ones. The males were much larger than the females. Sea elephants do not have legs and move by contracting and expanding their bodies like snakes. Given their weight, they cannot move fast, but they have huge teeth. I thought that I would not like to be caught by one of them. They came to incubate on this beach and during the incubation period they become dangerous. Visitors were forbidden to go all the way down to where they were. Some of the sea elephants were engaging in a weird rite: They were smashing against each other's chests with tremendous force while making strange, loud sounds. I could not tell whether they were playing or fighting. I quickly attracted their attention by dropping a small stone on some of them. They looked at me with an expression that was not exactly friendly. Their look seemed to say, "if I catch you, you are mine." I took several pictures while my wife worked on her video. It was a sight as alien as any I had ever seen.

After this excursion, we went back to the car and covered many more miles—more emptiness with occasionally great sights of fauna. We saw some splendid guanacos, a kind of wild llama. They are graceful and elegant and move in large groups. We saw some Patagonian rabbits, lots of sheep, and some *Rhea Americana*, a bird that does not fly and weighs about 30 kilos. We also saw lots of horses and many other animals. Península de Valdés is famous for its fauna, which is amazingly abundant. We stopped at a place not far from Puerto Deseado, where there was an incredibly beautiful view of the sea. The cliff fell sharply down at least 100 meters and, down by the sea, there were more sea elephants. But there was no path down to the beach and, in any case, the wind was so strong that I was afraid I would be pushed down the cliff.

We stopped at the only sign of civilization in the whole immense area, a restaurant and small hotel next to a light house, which we were told could be seen from 50 miles away: Punta Delgado. That is one of only a few light houses in Patagonia. We had a nice lunch—lamb, of course—and went to see other sea elephants within walking distance from the hotel. Once again, the beach was a long way below land level. Erosion had given a beautiful look to the whole coast line. However, given that the very high tides in this area (up to 8 meters), during low tides there is a huge, flat area by the beach on which one can walk. On this beach, there were also some sea lions and many sea elephants which, apparently, were not incubating and were less dangerous. The beach was extremely beautiful and different from any other beaches I had seen. It had strange rocks, lots of different aquariums formed among the rocks, algae of different colors, sea lions splashing in water, and so forth. On this beach one was allowed to walk. Once again, I invited some of these enormous monsters to show their teeth by dropping small stones on them. I figured that I could move faster than they could, but I kept a safe distance just in case. Soon, the weather became an actor once again. Within minutes, the sky was covered with clouds, thunder clapped, and huge drops of the coldest rain I had ever felt came down. The drops were mixed with small pieces of ice. We took refuge in a small abandoned construction, built apparently to house a "fauna guardian." After it was built, they must have realized that nobody, or almost nobody, came here or lived within 200 miles, so it was abandoned. Within a few minutes, the most splendid sun came out and we enjoyed the sight once again. The absence of pollution and humidity gave the light an unusual color.

After the visit to the sea elephants, we visited a small port, Puerto Pirámide, with a population of less than 100 people. It was the most important urban center in the area. Apparently, it is important for whale watching and it has some historical significance but, otherwise, this was the least interesting part of the trip.

Once back in the hotel in Puerto Madryn, we went for a walk around town, bought some herbal tea (they had several kinds and it was very cheap), sat outside a coffee shop for coffee, and returned to the hotel. At the hotel, Gustavo Díaz called from downstairs—he had brought several pictures he had taken during the boat ride before the storm. We appreciated this kind gesture. We went back for dinner to Mi Pequeño Restaurant and had a marvelous crab meat dinner with *salsa holandesa*.

Early the next morning, we went to see the penguin colony at Punta Tomba. It was the incubating season and most of the penguins were inside their holes warming their eggs. It had been estimated that there were about 700,000 penguins in this colony. Thus, it could be considered a Penguin metropolis. We were told that each penguin has its own kind of habitat, its own hole, which is almost a personal address, and they return there every year. It was very strange to walk in this penguin town and see the penguins sit on their eggs or move around totally indifferent to our presence. They were smaller than I thought they would be. We took lots of pictures, had "empanadas" at the little building that was a combination of souvenir shop and restaurant, and left for the airport. On our way there, we saw a large group of guanacos and tried to get close to them to take more pictures. However, they would move away as we tried to get closer. I also saw and photographed some Patagonian hares. Finally, I photographed about a thousand sheep. At the airport of Trelew, we saw a plaque dedicated to Antoine de St. Exupery and, on the plane, we talked to a large group of French tourists who were ecstatic about their trip. We concluded that Península de Valdés must be one of the most interesting destinations for tourists interested in nature and, especially, in a kind of fauna rarely seen even in documentaries.

We returned to Washington in early November. On a purely personal and sad note, Madeleine, my wife, enjoyed the trip a lot and seemed to have lots of energy the whole time. However, at that time she was very ill with breast cancer, which had spread to her bones and to other parts of her body. She had already exhausted the possibilities offered by chemotherapy and was taking Tamaxifen, a drug that slows down the spread of the disease. A few days after our return to Washington, she started complaining of strong headaches. Her physicians thought that she may have caught some virus during the trip, but tests soon revealed that the cancer had gone to the brain. We were told that she had no more than three months of life left. Unfortunately, the doctors' forecast proved accurate. She died on March 15, 1995.

CHAPTER VIII

The Approaching Storm

The year 1994 was the last truly good one for Argentina. The following year, 1995, brought a sharp recession: the GDP fell by 2.8 percent (after five years of high growth) and unemployment became a major worry. The fast rate of growth in the 1990–1994 period had not created many jobs. The privatization of public enterprises had allowed the new owners to shed about 40 percent of the workers. Moreover, high social security taxes on employers and rigid labor laws had not provided the needed flexibility to create new jobs. The privatization of enterprises, the railroad in particular, had led to cuts in services to some faraway areas. Several small towns had literally died when they were cut off from main economic centers. The rise in interest rates and in the value of the dollar—and the problems in Mexico and in Brazil—had contributed to the difficulties, but internal problems started to make themselves felt. Thus the possibility of a storm appeared over a house with weak foundations.

The relationship between Menem and Cavallo started to deteriorate. Cavallo's alledged ambition to become president, which started to be discussed publicly, must have collided with Menem's wish to continue in his position. There was increasing talk about corruption. Rumors about a possible financial crisis also started to be heard. There was concern about a "tequila effect" coming from the Mexican crisis. Tax revenue fell and the fiscal deficit rose to over 3 percent of GDP in spite of a strong but time-limited attempt to contain public spending. Although well received by the IMF, the attempt to contain spending, probably pushed by Cavallo, was described by Menem as "surgery without anesthesia." Doubts also began to appear about whether the official deficit estimates were comprehensive and correct. Mario Teijeiro, an Argentine economist who had worked in my department at the IMF before moving back to Argentina, and who had co-authored a paper with Mario Blejer and myself, started raising questions about the accuracy of the fiscal statistics. Teijeiro had done the difficult job of estimating the "true" fiscal deficit from the time when the Convertibility Law was enacted. In his conceptual framework, he had replaced cash concepts with accrual concepts. He had especially made adjustments for privatization revenue and for payments financed by the forced issuance of bonds ("bocones"). In 1996 he published a paper titled "La Politica Fiscal Durante la Convertibilidad" with his results. A problem was that some public spending was leading to higher public debt but was not reported in the budget and, thus, was not reflected in the official fiscal deficit. Some of this spending was commanded by decisions of the judiciary. In particular years, the differences in the deficit between the official and the IMF estimates and Teijero's estimates approached 2 percent of GDP. Teijeiro's estimates better reflected the growth in public debt. In 1995, unemployment reached levels perhaps never experienced before and concerns that Argentina might be moving toward a financial crisis like Mexico's grew. Suddenly, Argentina had gone from being a miracle country or an economic tiger to one under close observation.

On August 2, 1995 Carlos Tacchi suddenly resigned from his job as revenue secretary and was replaced by Ricardo Gutiérrez. The reason for Tacchi's resignation was the political pressures he was receiving to give tax preferences and to turn a blind eye to some questionable tax practices. In one case, for example, he had insisted on fully taxing the wholesale importation of cars by a prominent supporter of Menem. Cavallo had criticized Tacchi for being too rigid. However, instead of apologizing, Tacchi reacted sharply and publicly and Cavallo backed down. The economic crisis heightened tensions and the potential rivalry between Menem and Cavallo started to attract public attention. It was reported that Cavallo had wanted to succeed Menem in the presidency of Argentina but the Constitutional reform of 1994 had allowed Menem's reelection in 1995. This had ruined the chance for Cavallo and had intensified their rivalry. Cavallo would soon leave the Menem administration.

On August 10, 1995 I got a call from Argentina informing me that President Menem, probably as a reaction to Tacchi's resignation a week earlier, would appear on TV that afternoon to announce some new measures against tax evasion. I was asked to give an opinion on whether the measures made sense. After some consultation with my colleagues in the Fiscal Affairs Department, I called back to say that the measures were likely to be ineffective for a long time. I was told, "sorry but President Menem needs to make a statement." Thus the speech was made and most newspapers the next day reported that measures against tax evasion were being taken.

Given the Convertibility Law and the sharp appreciation of the dollar (and of the peso that was tied to it), prices in Argentina became very high. Buenos Aires became a very expensive city. There were increasing concerns about the survival of the convertibility system and many observers were calling for its elimination, which meant letting the peso fluctuate (and lose value) with respect to the dollar and other currencies. At the IMF, we had an interdepartmental meeting on the topic and representatives from the Research Department expressed a preference for freeing the exchange rate. I expressed my concern that, given the fiscal deficit and the rising public debt, this change could bring back high inflation as in the 1980s. In my view, removing the anchor provided by the Convertibility Law in a country that had experienced very high inflation for fifty years, because of its continuous recourse to the Central Bank to finance its fiscal deficit, would be the same as opening the drug closet for a drug addict. After all, the goal of Argentina's Central Bank was to keep the currency stable. I also felt that it would have been impossible to abandon the fixed exchange rate without also reneging on the foreign debt, which by that time had become significant. Devaluation would considerably increase the cost in pesos of servicing the foreign debt and would not have helped in reducing the fiscal deficit. No consensus on what position the Fund should take was reached at the meeting.

In March 1996, I went back to Buenos Aires, directly after a visit to Israel. The purpose of my visit to Argentina was to be part of a roundtable at the Annual Meeting of the InterAmerican Development Bank, which was taking place in Buenos Aires that year. The roundtable would discuss the idea of creating National Fiscal Councils, an idea pushed by Ricardo Hausmann, then the chief economist at the IDB, and by other well-known economists such as Barry Eichengreen and Jurgen von Hagen. These councils would be national institutions with the power to establish limits to the public debts of different countries. They would be politically independent, like some central banks, and would have the final word on macroeconomic aspects of fiscal policy. Hausmann was worried about the growth of public debt in many Latin American countries at that time and the potential consequences of it. He believed that by depoliticizing fiscal decisions, and giving the final say to a group of technically competent and politically independent individuals without any lobby to satisfy, these National Fiscal Councils would lead to better fiscal outcomes. The panel would be chaired by Jacob Frenkel, who had been head of the Research Department at the IMF and was then governor of the Central Bank of Israel. Ricardo

Hausmann would make a presentation of the main idea, stressing its merits, and the panel would discuss it.

The panel consisted of Guillermo Ortíz, then deputy minister of finance in Mexico; José Serra, then minister of industry in Brazil and later a candidate for the Brazilian presidency; Larry Summers, then undersecretary in the U.S. Treasury; and myself. Everyone went after Hausmann's idea pointing out that: fiscal decisions are the most political decisions that governments make; that parliaments would never agree to withdraw from political decisions that are typically their responsibility; that the appointment of the members of the councils would become as contentious as those for the U.S. Supreme Court; that council members would not be free from the pressures created by lobbies; that macro fiscal outcomes are the result of many micro fiscal decisions that would still be made by parliaments; and that, when the chips were down, the decisions of the councils would be ignored, as it happened in many Latin American countries with the constitutional laws that required budget balance; or the decisions would be reinterpreted to make them useless as it has happened with the Italian Constitution.

I was the last to speak and many of the points I had wanted to make had already been made by those who had spoken before me. Thus, I started my intervention by comparing myself with Elizabeth Taylor's eighth husband on their first night together. He knew what he was expected to do, the problem was how to make it interesting. I got a big laugh from the nearly five hundred people in the audience. The next day, some newspapers referred to my speech saying that it proved that the IMF could have a sense of humor, a characteristic not often attributed to the institution. In any case, the consensus of the panel was that, in spite of its academic appeal, the idea of the National Fiscal Councils was unrealistic.

After the meeting I met Carlos Tacchi for lunch. By this time, he had been out of the government for seven months. We went to Galerías Pacifico, a newly opened and elegant shopping mall on Calle Florida, which was located in a building that had belonged to the Argentine Railroad. During my many visits to Argentina over the years, I had often paid attention to that building because of its location, the beauty of its exterior and the fact that, except for a couple of rooms on the ground floor, it had been empty for years. The building had been badly in need of repairs but the railroad did not have the funds to repair it. So it was just left vacant and in a deteriorating state. One time, in the late 1980s, I was invited to give a talk at the Buenos Aires Bolsa de Comercio (Stock Exchange). The talk was attended by a large audience. I used the example of that building to argue that public assets should be used productively. The "misuse of public assets" was a topic that had interested me for some time and it would be the subject of a paper I wrote that would have a significant policy impact, especially in Italy. I argued that if the state, or the public enterprises, do not have the means to put their assets to the best use, they should sell them and let the private sector do it. This would increase the country's income and tax revenue. This was a form of privatization that had not received much attention because all the attention in the privatization debate had gone to the public enterprises.

When the railroad was privatized, the new owners sold this building, thus increasing both Argentina's income and taxes. Unfortunately, the process of privatization was not as transparent as it should have been. A general perception in Argentina is that there was corruption when assets were transferred from public to private hands. It was widely believed that, in some cases, the buyers had paid less than they should have paid for the public assets, and had received more monopoly power over their future use than it would have been desirable. These advantages might have been obtained by making side payments (paying bribes) to particular individuals or political groups. *Robo para la corona* (stealing for the crown) is the title of a popular book on corruption written by Horacio Verbitsky. The title came from a statement attributed to a minister in the Menem administration to the effect that, if there had been corruption in the privatization process, it would be condonable because it was "stealing for the crown." By this time, Cavallo seemed to be in open conflict with Menem and had started mentioning with increasing frequency the problem of corruption within the Menem administration. Cavallo believed that there was a kind of mafia that was engaging in various acts of corruption.

After lunch, Tacchi and I paid a visit to Martínez de Hoz, the former minister of economy, in his apartment near the Plaza Hotel. He lived in one of the first skyscrapers built in Latin America, another sign of Argentina's prominence in the first half of the last century. He was happy to see us; I had not seen him since 1978, when he was still in the government. After the visit, Tacchi and I went for a walk around the center of Buenos Aires and I was surprised by the number of people who recognized Tacchi and came to greet him, telling him how much they missed his integrity and good work. For a former tax collector, this was a great compliment. He had obviously remained popular after his resignation for not getting the government's full support in his fight against tax evasion. We spent a lot of time talking about corruption, which by this time had become a hot topic in Buenos Aires. Because at the time I was writing on the subject and pushing Mr. Camdessus and the IMF to become more active and outspoken in the fight against corruption, I was interested in learning as much as I could about this phenomenon in Argentina (on May 7, 1995 an article in *La Nación* newspaper referred to my work on corruption). I asked Tacchi if there were books on the topic published in Argentina and he promised to send me some. That evening, when I returned to the hotel to prepare for my departure, I found a package with five or six recently published books on corruption in Argentina. These books included the above-mentioned book by Horacio Verbitsky and *Pizza con Champán: Crónica de la Fiesta Menemista* by Sylvina Walger.

I was surprised upon receiving these books because I had not heard much discussion of this problem in Washington. This strengthened my view that if the IMF wanted to play a useful role in Argentina, and in several similar countries, it should redirect some of its attention from collecting precise but potentially contaminated statistics to issues such as governance and transparency that, over the long run, would determine the success or failure of Argentina's and other countries' policies. Focusing only on macroeconomic numbers, as some insisted that the IMF should do, was like trying to understand what is happening on the ground while looking down from a plane flying at 10,000 meters high. The question of the transparency of the fiscal accounts, a separate issue from that of corruption, would become a major topic in later years, when the real size of the fiscal deficit was discussed in Argentina, and within the Fund. How to treat the revenue from privatization and the payments of old debts to pensioners would become hot issues. In the meantime, the public debt kept growing and much of it was financed from abroad.

I went back to Argentina a few weeks later to participate in the Fourth Tributary Congress given by the "Consejo Profesional de Ciencias Económicas de la Capital Federal." This "Consejo" is a powerful institution with a membership, at that time, of 44,000 people. It even owned a rather large building in the center of Buenos Aires. In addition to myself, Professor Addonino from the University of Rome, a tax lawyer who was then president of the International Fiscal

Association, and three Spanish fiscal experts were also participating in the congress from outside Argentina. The night of my arrival in Buenos Aires, I was invited to give a public lecture on globalization and taxation at the headquarters of the Consejo. The lecture was well attended. I was quite sleepy because of the overnight flight but did a reasonable job in my delivery. After the lecture, the foreign guests were taken to a nice restaurant in the new area by the port called Puerto Madero, which was becoming one of the booming and nicest areas of Buenos Aires. Privatization of previously "misused assets," plus some smart money from abroad, had transformed an area that had been populated mainly by rats to one patronized by the chic inhabitants of Buenos Aires. The old and long-abandoned customs warehouses by the port, which had been important for storing goods for export or import in the earlier part of the past century, had become fancy shops, offices, and expensive apartments. This again was an example of putting public assets that had been misused (in this case abandoned for decades) to economically good use, thus generating incomes and tax revenue. But, once again, the transfer of property titles was probably less transparent than desirable. The restaurant was called "Dique Cuatro." It was very good and very expensive. I figured that, at that time, it would be difficult to find a more expensive restaurant in Washington.

The combination of the increasingly overvalued exchange rate, the higher national income created by several years of high growth, and the progressively more uneven distribution of income, were creating the conditions for these high priced and high quality restaurants to exist. Some Argentines were doing very well and were able to patronize these places while unemployment was rampant and poverty was increasing. Cavallo had hoped to prevent the appreciation of the peso by keeping the inflation rate in Argentina below the world rate, but this had proved difficult, except in 1996, in part because of rigidities in the labor market and large increases in wages. It had not been politically possible for a Peronist government to pass laws that would make the labor market more flexible. Since the start of the convertibility plan on April 1, 1991, the consumer price index had increased by almost 50 percent (by 1994). This happened with a fixed exchange rate.

By this time, Argentina had started to show clear signs of the two factors that would eventually lead to the crisis of 2001: an appreciating exchange rate and an accumulation of foreign public debt. Especially in relation to Argentina's exports, the debt had become very large. Of course, the more debt it accumulated abroad, the more costly, in domestic currency, would that debt become in case of a devaluation. A devaluation would sharply increase the ratio of foreign debt (normally denominated in dollars) to GDP and would not solve the fiscal problem. If the devaluation were accompanied by the introduction of a flexible exchange rate regime, and if Argentina continued to run a significant fiscal deficit, as it had been doing, the probability that it would go back to the inflationary habits of the past would be substantial. For these reasons, I remained unconvinced that the abandonment of the Convertibility Law (which had allowed Argentina's citizens to exchange pesos for U.S. dollars at the rate of one to one) could be a solution to the growing foreign debt. This, of course, did not mean that under current policies the Convertibility Law was likely to be maintained forever. The solution, if there were one, could only have come from a substantial adjustment in the fiscal accounts. Argentina would have another window of opportunity in the three years after the recession of 1995, when growth would resume at a significant pace. But, unfortunately, it would not exploit that opportunity.

The Fourth Public Finance Congress was going to be held in Mendoza, a very Italian city that produces some of Argentina's best wine. So the morning after my arrival, I took a 7:00 a.m. flight to Mendoza. The flight lasted about one hour and a half, after which I was taken to the Hotel Aconcagua. The name of the hotel comes from Mount Aconcagua in the Andes, one of the world's highest range of mountains. Aconcagua is about 7,000 meters high and considered one of the big challenges for climbers. I was told that, on average, five to six climbers die each year in the attempt to climb it. I also learned that the son of an old acquaintance of mine had died on this mountain a few years earlier. He fell in a crevasse and his body was never recovered.

The two main themes for the congress were: "tax structure and globalized economy" and "the concept of world income." I had drafted a few notes on the determinants of tax structures, identifying factors such as the structure of the economy, the need for revenue, per capita income, and so forth. I thought that I was stating the obvious but my lecture was well received and was even reported in the newspapers the following day. I was inevitably drawn into a discussion on Argentine economy. For good or bad reasons, I had acquired visibility in Argentina and was invited to speak in a radio program and interviewed by reporters. I used the opportunity to send a message to the authorities in a non-abrasive way. The message was: if you cannot cut spending, you must raise taxes. If you need to raise taxes, consider raising the personal income tax that is the tax base most underused in Argentina. At that time, the personal income tax was generating less than 1 percent of GDP. *Clarín, El Cronista,* and *Página 12,* all published interviews in which I called for a strengthening of the fiscal effort and for more taxation on income and wealth. I tried to add humor to my warning stating that "wise men learn from other men's mistakes; however, in the process they deprive themselves of the excitement and the adventure of making the mistakes themselves."

After talking to several of the participants at this meeting, I had the clear impression that the mood had changed even though the economy was recovering well from the 1995 recession. The "fiesta Menemista" was showing signs of fatigue. In part, this was the result of the deep recession in the previous months; the sharp increase in the unemployment rate, which had jumped from 7–8 percent in 1988–1992, to about 10 percent in 1993–1994, and to 17–18 percent in 1995–1996; and the frequent talk about corruption. With such rates of unemployment it became progressively more difficult to talk about economic success, regardless of the rate of economic growth which would return to be significantly positive in 1996 (5.5 percent), 1997 (8.1 percent), and 1998 (3.8 percent). By this time, Domingo Cavallo had lost some of his prestige and clout, doubts had appeared about the economic strategy, and questions were raised on whether Argentina would be able to maintain the convertibility of the peso into dollars at the fixed exchange rate. Tax revenue was down; the fight against tax evasion had become less fierce with Tacchi's departure; and the government was relying more and more on foreign loans, which continued to be available. The clouds for a big storm were forming and becoming quite visible to close observers. In July 1996, Cavallo was replaced by Roque Fernández as economy minister. I would see Cavallo a couple of months after his resignation at the meeting of the American Economic Association in New Orleans. He would give a talk that was critical of the IMF because it had not enthusiastically endorsed the Convertibility Law, and had expressed doubts from the beginning.

Meanwhile, corruption had become a topic of frequent conversation. At that time, Aldo Dadone, the president of Banco de la Nación, was in trouble due to some dealings with IBM and the common assumption was that he might end in jail. I had met him during the tax mission in August 1989. He was the author of the paper that suggested that a single tax on transactions could replace all the existing taxes without any revenue loss and with increased efficiency! In recent years, he had divorced his wife and married a young woman. I noticed a correlation between accusations of corruption and recycling with young wives. But (a common problem in economics), I could not decide which was the cause and which the effect.

During this trip I read in the newspapers that, for the first time in the history of Argentina, judges had actually sentenced a tax evader to jail. He was accused of not reporting millions of pesos to the tax authorities. However, I also learned that the Argentine Supreme Court had confirmed a lower court interpretation of the Constitution, through which judges could not be taxed on their salaries. These were the same guys that would apply harsh penalties to tax evaders. Furthermore, until recently, judges had had good company in their special tax-free status: legislators had also been tax free. The newspapers reported that it had taken thirty-four legislative proposals to eliminate the tax free status for these officials. This information helped me understand why it had been so difficult to have a significant personal income tax in Argentina.

In Mendoza, I was invited to dinner by Ana M. Mosso, a high official in the local government. We went to a restaurant called Trevi ("il ristorante italiano di Mendoza"), which was run by a charming man from Marche, a region in central Italy. The food was truly Italian and very good. The owner, who was happy to speak to an Italian, told me that Mendoza was populated mostly by Italians, or by descendants of Italians. In fact, everyone I met there seemed to have an Italian name. During dinner, I learned a lot about the finances of the local governments. For example, in the province of Mendoza there was no inventory of public assets. The government did not know what it owned. This is not as strange as it sounds; many governments do not have this information. Local officials were exempt from many taxes or fees such as those on water, electricity, and other services. The controls on public expenditure were very weak. I could not help but think about the World Bank's campaign at that time to push for fiscal decentralization in most countries. This would transfer power to institutions that were not prepared for it. In fact, a good part of Argentina's public finance problems had to do with the inability to control the spending of sub-national governments. A constant in the economic policy of Argentina over the previous decades, and especially during the Alfonsín period, had been the attempt by the central government to cut public spending and public employment while that effort was routinely neutralized by the actions of the provincial governments.

I learned that, in the province of Mendoza, the penalty for tax evasion was only 10 percent *of the tax owed*. In some serious cases, they might close a shop for three days putting a sign on the door that announced that the shop had been closed because of tax evasion. Ana told me that, in one case, in order to hide the embarrassment that came with closure, someone had tried to cover the entrance to the shop with construction screens. There were also many exemptions that made the tax system look like Swiss cheese. For property taxes, the exemptions eliminated most of the tax base. The low assessment of the property value eliminated the rest of the tax base. The stamp tax was related to the value reported in the documents. The result was that there was a big incentive to undervalue.

Concerns about the fiscal situation and, especially, about falling public sector revenue induced the new economy minister, Roque Fernández, to ask the IMF to allow Carlos Silvani, who had been working in the Fund's Fiscal Affairs Department, to become Argentina's director of taxation. This request was unusual for at least two reasons: First, Silvani had recently led a Fund mission to Argentina on tax administration, which had been critical of developments. His report had elicited a rather sharp response from the Argentine authorities. Second, IMF rules forbade Fund employees to occupy executive positions in the governments of their countries of origin without resigning from the Fund. But enough pressure was applied on Fund management to allow Silvani to go to Argentina while still technically an employee of the IMF. He left his family in Washington. This was an indication of the deterioration of the fiscal situation, at least as seen from Buenos Aires. Between 1994 and 1996, the deficit of the public sector, measured on an accrual basis, had increased by well over 3 percent of GDP. After some fall in 1997, it would increase again doubling the 1996 level by 2001. Silvani moved to Argentina in October 1996 and remained there as director of taxation and then as revenue secretary until June 2000, when he returned to Washington. During his time in Buenos Aires, tax revenue rose by about 2 percent of GDP, but sharp increases in public spending and reductions in social security contributions resulted in the deterioration of the fiscal situation and the increase in external public debt.

Silvani would try hard to increase revenue significantly but found that various obstacles (including problems in the judiciary) made it difficult for him to succeed. The fact that a Fund employee was in charge of the revenue side of the national budget, in some sense, made the Fund share in the responsibility of fiscal developments. It made it more difficult for the IMF to claim that it had an arm's length relationship with a major customer.

I went back to Buenos Aires in December 1996 accompanied by Teresa Ter Minassian, then deputy director of the Fiscal Affairs Department, who was in the process of transferring to the Western Hemisphere Department. I had come to open a seminar on fiscal federalism at the Central Bank and to discuss the developments of the fiscal accounts which continued to worry. The fiscal deficit, adjusted for off-budget expenditures for 1996, would be estimated at 4 percent of GDP by the IMF and at 5.5 percent of GDP by Mario Teijeiro. The new economy minister, Roque Fernández was worried enough by the deficit to decide to postpone the payment of the extra salaries, usually paid in December, to the following year. This, of course, would complicate the accounts for 1997. The deficit for 1996 would be substantially above the level that had been agreed with the Fund. Various newspapers reported my worries and statements of the fact that, without some fiscal adjustment, it would be difficult for the IMF to agree on the extension of its lending program the following February. There was some hope that the arrival of Carlos Silvani two months earlier would help.

At the time of this visit, the question of ethics in government was being hotly debated. The vice president in the Menem administration, Carlos Ruckauf, at the opening of the Primeras Jornadas Sobre Ética Pública (First Conference on Public Ethics), recognized that the question of a clean government was a "central demand of the Argentine society." He and Carlos Corach, the interior minister, announced the creation of an office of ethics as an answer to the corruption problems. This office would be similar to the one created by the Clinton administration in Washington, and would be under the control of the interior ministry. Mr. Stephen Potts, head of the Office of Public Ethics in Washington, was invited to Buenos Aires for advice. He recommended that the office should not just try to prevent corruption but also investigate acts of corruption, including those suspected by ministers. Clearly this was a topic that was becoming progressively hotter.

In August 1997, I went back to Argentina for two reasons: First to receive an honorary degree from the University of Córdoba; and second to join for a couple of days a tax mission from my department headed by Partho Shome. The mission had been requested by Roque Fernández, the new economy minister. The Argentine authorities were thinking of introducing some significant tax changes and wanted the Fund's views on these changes, as well as the Fund's experts' estimations of what impact the changes would have on tax revenue. The ceremony for the granting of the degree and the tax mission had been timed so that I could combine both activities in the same trip. In Buenos Aires, I was surprised by how cheap taxis were compared to almost anything else. One reason was liberalization, which had reduced the entrance costs into this activity. The second was the cloning of registered taxis. Perfect copies of registered taxis with fake registrations had increased the supply of taxis, which seemed to be half the cars on the streets. This development had also increased the risks for passengers. Kidnapping for a quick ransom was becoming common.

The proposal for the degree had originated with Professor Ernesto Rezk, the public finance professor at the University of Córdoba and the person who had chaired the local committee for the 1989 meeting in Buenos Aires of the International Institute of Public Finance. It had been quickly endorsed by the university's rector, in spite of the fact that I was a Fund employee and, I was told, he had Marxist leanings. I flew overnight to Buenos Aires, changed in a hotel room rented just for this purpose, and then got back on a plane to fly to Cordoba. I got there just in time for the highly formal ceremony, held in a sixteenth-century hall that could have been in an Italian or Spanish city from that period. I was surprised by how European Renaissance or early Baroque the center of Cordoba was. I learned that the University of Córdoba had been founded in 1613, two decades before Harvard. It was the second oldest university on the continental part of the Americas after San Carlos of Antigua in Guatemala. The University of Santo Domingo in the Dominican Republic is the oldest one in the Americas.

After the various introductory speeches and my formal lecture, there was a reception during which I was interviewed by some reporters interested in my views on Argentine economic and, especially, fiscal developments. I took the opportunity to caution again about the trend in the public finances. In 1997, the public sector of Argentina had to sell 6.4 percent of GDP in public bonds, to replace maturing debt and to cover the deficit, while the "country risk" was rising sharply, making the financing of the deficit and the servicing of the public debt progressively more expensive. The developing crisis of South East Asia, which was at its very beginning, and difficulties in Brazil were not helping. Still, this was a year when the Argentine economy was growing at a very high rate and it should not be having fiscal problems.

Before leaving Córdoba for Buenos Aires, I was invited to lunch by Governor de la Sota, the provincial governor who was being mentioned at that time as a potential successor to Menem. From him, I heard some views on the provincial finances. At the time, he was making news for having reduced the tax rates while tax revenues for the province had increased. However, it turned out that the revenue increase had come from changes which had nothing to do with rate reductions and the Laffer curve. Still this governor seemed to be considering a reduction in the economic role of the state, which I endorsed. He requested some Fund assistance with reforming the tax administration. Even though the Fund usually assisted only national governments, I agreed to consider the request and a Fund mission was sent some time later.

In Buenos Aires, I joined the Shome's mission for the final discussions with the authorities. The authorities were considering the following changes to the tax system: First, the reduction of social security taxes on employers to reduce the cost of labor and, hopefully, to reduce unemployment. This measure would be a substitute for the failure to reform labor laws, a reform continually asked by the IMF. This measure would be costly in terms of revenue and thus create more difficulties for the public finances. To compensate for this revenue loss, they were considering changes with a positive impact on tax revenue. Second, to reduce the large personal exemption for the income tax on individuals. The existing exemption was so high that it eliminated a large part of the tax base, making the personal income tax a highly unproductive tax. Third, to increase the excise taxes on diesel in order to bring them closer to those on gasoline. Diesel was lightly taxed because it was used in agriculture but many expensive cars were using it. Finally, for the enterprises, to disallow the deductions they took for the large borrowing they made, while, at the same time, to exempt the interest income they received. Iceland had done something along this line. Debt had largely replaced equity in the financing of enterprises. A simple method for enterprises to reduce taxes was for their owners to bring their money off shore and to lend that money, through some intermediary, to their own enterprises so they could get a tax free return on their investments. In this way, the interest payment by the enterprise was fully deductible while the income paid in the form of interest payments was tax free. The result was that taxes on enterprises generated very little revenue.

The proposal by the Argentine authorities to reduce the social security taxes represented a continuation of their attempts to get around structural problems faced by the economy with manipulations of the tax system. These attempts were not in the spirit of the 1989 tax reform that had changed the Argentine tax system. Over the following years, these attempts would become more frequent and more convoluted. They would not be coordinated with those who were responsible for administering the tax system and would inevitably affect the administration and the compliance of the tax system. In the meeting with Roque Fernández and his colleagues, we focused on the fact that the reduction of the contributions that employers made to the pension system could cost, in lost revenue, as much as 1.4 percent of GDP. This large loss would come completely *from the budget of the central government*. On the other hand, given the fact that most taxes collected by the central government were legally shared with the provinces, and that the sharing was generally about fifty-fifty, the central government would need to raise about twice the 1.4 percent of GDP that it would lose from the social security change in order to have a neutral impact on its budget. The provinces always spent all they got. It would be very difficult, if not impossible, to raise close to 3 percent of GDP from other taxes.

During this meeting, Roque Fernández, who had been a visiting scholar in the Fiscal Affairs Department of the IMF, and Pablo Guidotti, the treasury secretary, who had been on the staff of the Fund's Research Department, expressed some concern about a major public project that was being contemplated at that time by some of the ministers in the Menem administration. The project, which would require huge spending, concerned the construction of a "trans-American highway," which would connect Argentina to the Pacific coast of South America. This project was being contemplated at a time when interest rates were rising sharply and Argentina was negotiating a large loan with the IMF. It was obvious that, while Roque Fernández and his team saw the IMF loan as an insurance against potential future negative developments, given the fungeability of money some in the Menem administration may have seen the loan as an opportunity for politically attractive public spending. On my return to Washington, I informed the managing director of the IMF about this plan and this set in motion a process to stop the project. This episode, however, confirmed my view that, while the Fund continued to see its loans to Argentina as supporting policies aimed at reducing the dangers faced by the Argentine economy, at least some in the Menem administration saw the money as a cheap resource that made it possible for the government to maintain or even increase the high level of public spending. Fund credit was clearly the cheapest source of financing public spending at that time.

By August 1997, I had become very concerned about fiscal developments in Argentina. In spite of the economy's high rate of growth (5.5 in 1996 and 8.1 in 1997); in spite of a highly capable group of individuals in the key economic positions of economy minister, treasury secretary, and revenue secretary; and in spite of the fact that tax revenue had increased significantly in real terms, if not as a share of GDP, the fiscal deficit and the public debt were still rising. Furthermore, the not so ambitious fiscal deficit targets agreed with the Fund had been exceeded every year since 1994. The public debt was largely foreign and had to be serviced at interest rates that were becoming progressively higher. I saw dark clouds on the horizon and made no secret about my views, both within and outside the IMF. I began to think that it would be unwise for the Fund to continue to make money available to Argentina, because this could only result in the country's increase in foreign debt, which could lead to major problems. I saw no signs of adjustments in the economy and in its fiscal accounts that would have justified financial assistance from the IMF.

Before leaving Buenos Aires, I was interviewed by various leading newspapers, including *La Nación, Clarín, Página 12, El Cronista, BAE*, and others. In these interviews, I clearly expressed my worries and my view that a fiscal adjustment was necessary. By this time, I was convinced that it would be very difficult to reduce public spending, given the preferences of the government and the legal arrangements that left to the sub-national governments much of the power to spend. The political power of the provincial governments and the existing revenue sharing arrangements were a major contributing factor to the macroeconomic difficulties that would be faced by Argentina. Thus, I stressed the need to increase the level of taxation *but not through special taxes*. I kept insisting that the rich in Argentina, of whom were many at that time, should pay some personal income taxes because, in comparison with other countries, they were paying almost nothing. The personal income tax had been traditionally a very underused source of revenue in Argentina.

At this point, a curious problem of internal governance at the IMF started to appear: Because I would spend the last three months of 1997 away from the Fund, on a sabbatical leave in Budapest, I would not notice the problem fully until I returned to the Fund in 1998. The problem was that I started to be cut out of important IMF meetings that dealt with Argentina. This kind of governance problem was possible at the IMF because of the amorphous and opaque rules concerning the presence of department heads at key meetings and at decision-making sessions at the institution. This opacity gives some individuals the possibility of playing games by not informing about, or not inviting particular individuals to significant meetings. This was especially the case when the latter might raise objections to courses of action that those who called the meetings would like to pursue. Perhaps, the management of the Western Hemisphere Department, which by this time had new individuals at the top, felt that it no longer needed the views on Argentina's fiscal developments from the director of the Fiscal Affairs Department. Or, perhaps, they assumed that those views were well known. Or perhaps, but less likely, the signals came from higher up, from the office of a deputy managing director. This was a peculiar situation because of my long involvement with Argentina and because, as a report of the Independent Evaluation Office of the IMF would later state: "Fiscal policy was the single most prominent topic of discussion between the IMF and the Argentine authorities for virtually the entire period of convertibility" (see page 37 of the "Report on the Evaluation of the Role of the IMF in Argentina, 1991–2001" [June 30, 2004]).

CHAPTER IX

The End of the "Fiesta Menemista"

After the 1997 Annual Meetings of the Fund and the World Bank in Hong Kong, which took place in September, I took advantage of a sabbatical program that the Fund allowed its professional staff to take once during their career. An IMF economist could take a sabbatical leave of up to one year to teach at a university or to join a research institution. The obligation was to return to the Fund for three years afterward. Because I could not leave the department I directed for a full year, I asked for a three-month leave to teach at Colegium Budapest, Institute of Advanced Studies, in Budapest. This is a small multi-disciplinary institute shaped after the famous one in Princeton. I would be part of a small group of economists, coordinated by Prof. Janos Kornai, a prominent Hungarian economist. I traveled to Budapest at the end of September accompanied by my new wife, Maria. We had married the morning of September 30 and took a plane to Hungary that same afternoon.

Each visitor to Colegium Budapest was expected to give a public lecture based on a paper written during the time spent at the institute. Because of my strong interest at the time in the implications of corruption in a country's economy, I agreed with Prof. Kornai that my research and lecture would be on that subject. Thus, I wrote the first draft of a paper called "Corruption Around the World," which I gave as the required public lecture. At the time I was writing this paper in Budapest, I read a story published in the *Financial Times*, which reported that the president of Kenya had had an airport built with public money near his native village. This was a classic example of the "abuse of public power for private gains," the common definition of corruption used by the World Bank. I used the example in my article but, given the sensitivities of the Fund, I omitted the name of the country.

On my return to Washington, in early 1998, I revised and edited the paper and issued it in the *Working Paper* series of the IMF. These working papers are supposed to reflect the personal views of the authors—as they specifically state on the cover page—and, thus, do not necessarily reflect official IMF views. In theory, the authors are free to express their own opinions without the censorship of the IMF.

In practice, of course, most staff members are aware of implicit limits and exercise a lot of self-censorship. Occasionally, nervous supervisors, or even Fund, management, have intervened to stop papers that, in their judgment, could embarrass some important country. Not infrequently, the executive directors of particular countries have applied pressure to stop particular papers dealing with their countries, or to at least require revisions in an acceptable direction. For example, papers dealing with the taxation of petroleum would be stopped by the executive director of Saudi Arabia.

As a department director with a lot of seniority, I had far more freedom with my own papers, and especially with papers that dealt with fiscal issues. So on research papers dealing with fiscal issues I took the position that I was the "ultimate authority" at the IMF. Still, there were a few occasions over the years when I felt the need to consult or to discuss a planned paper with the managing director. Once, the managing director stopped a paper on tax reform in the United States. Another time, in a somewhat amusing case, a deputy managing director tried to stop a paper on money laundering that I had written and that had already received the full and enthusiastic endorsement of the managing director of the IMF. However, there had been no need for consultation regarding the paper I wrote in Budapest. It dealt with a general issue and not with a specific country. In time, that paper was published as the lead article in the Fund's academic journal, the *IMF Staff Papers*, and would be widely cited outside the IMF. In 2002 and 2003, it even made a list of the twenty-five most downloaded economic papers in the U.S.

One morning in 1998, a few days after the working paper had been issued, I got a very excited call from Guillermo Zoccali, then the executive director representing Argentina on the Board of the IMF. He was a nice and competent man and we had been good friends during the time we had both been at the IMF. We had always maintained cordial relations, even when he thought I had been too critical of Argentine fiscal developments, which at that time was happening more and more frequently. That morning, however, he seemed to be very upset and uncharacteristically brusque. He did not greet me and his first question was "how I could have done it." I asked what he was talking about but he kept repeating how I could have done this to Argentina, a country with which I had always had a close relationship. As he kept talking, I was reminded of Kafka's *Trial*, in which someone is arrested and brought for trial without being told what he is being tried for. Guillermo finally mentioned my paper on corruption saying that I should not have said what I said about President Menem. I was totally perplexed. I told him that I could not understand what he was talking about because the paper he mentioned did not deal with Argentina and, in fact, it never mentioned Argentina or President Menem. It took me some time to understand what had happened; I would have been amused by it if Guillermo had not been so upset.

By a strange coincidence, at the time when my working paper was issued the Argentine press was full of stories about corruption and, especially, about an airport President Menem was having built with public money in his small native town of Anillaco, in the province of La Rioja. A well-known political TV show ran by four well-known journalists had brought the issue of the Anillaco airport to the attention of the public creating a great political furor that led to the cancellation of the show. The fact that, at this time, Menem was toying with the idea of running again for president in 1999, in spite of the constitutional ban, made this accusation of corruption a politically explosive issue.

The airport could not be economically justified in a town of less than 1,000 inhabitants, so it was seen by the press as a clear act of corruption, even though the government claimed that it was difficult for the president to visit his hometown. Given my long-term relationship with Argentina, and my visibility in the country, when the Argentine reporters became aware of my working paper, they automatically assumed that the example of the airport built by the president of a country could only refer to Menem's airport. This conclusion was reported in Argentine newspapers. Both *La Nación* and *Clarín*, the two leading newspapers, published full-page articles referring to my paper on May 28 and May 26, respectively.

Zoccali refused to accept my explanation that the airport example had come from a *Financial Times* story about Kenya and that it had nothing to do with Argentina. He said that it was too much of a coincidence. Like Sherlock Holmes he did not believe in coincidences.

A short time after my telephone conversation with Zoccali, I got a call from the Argentine Embassy and was told that the Argentine ambassador to Washington, Mr. Diego Guelar, wanted to visit me as soon as possible. We arranged an early meeting and he soon appeared in my office at the IMF. The ambassador and I had the same discussion I had had with Zoccali. He could not believe either that my example did not come from Argentina. He once again repeated that I had always been considered a friend of Argentina and my actions were difficult to understand. After some discussion and my explanation of what had actually happened, he asked whether I would be willing to sign a declaration that stated that the example of the airport did not come from Argentina but from an African country, and that it had been reported a few months earlier by the *Financial Times*. Since this was the truth, I agreed to sign the statement. The ambassador asked whether I would have any objections to the statement being distributed to the Argentine press. I replied that I did not have any objections. The next morning, May 30, 1998, several Argentine newspapers reported the statement I had signed. However, some accompanied it by comments criticizing me for having given in to what they assumed had been pressures from the government. They simply joined the government in refusing to accept my explanation. At that time, I was completely unaware of what was going on in Argentina. I eventually found out from newspaper articles.

When the newspaper articles were published in late May, Menem was on official state visit to Finland accompanied by Guido Di Tella, the minister of foreign affairs. Menem was upset by the newspaper stories and Di Tella tried to contact Mr. Camdessus, the Fund's managing director, to complain and demand an explanation. However, Camdessus was also traveling and Di Tella was not able to reach him. Thus, he called the Argentine director at the Fund, Guillermo Zoccali, and the Argentine ambassador. My reply to the complaint was reported as an apology and not as an explanation. The title of the article in *La Nación* that reported my reply was "Disculpas de Tanzi a Menem" (apologies from Tanzi to Menem). In other words, nobody believed in my explanation.

Although at that time I was not fully aware of it, the sensitivity of the government to the publication of my article was also heightened by two other developments. *Transparency International* (TI), the international institution with headquarters in Berlin dedicated to the fight against corruption, had, a few months earlier, published its Corruption Perception Index (CPI) for 1997. The index had been launched in 1995 and it aimed at measuring the "perception" that international business interests and financial journalists had on corruption in their countries. The best score (i.e., the lowest perception of corruption) that a country could have was 10; the worst score was 1. For Argentina the index had shown a precipitous fall between 1995 and 1997: it had fallen from 5.24 to 2.81. A fall of 2.43

points in two years was *very* large, possibly larger than for any other country. The 1997 level of the index placed Argentina at the 42nd place among fifty-two countries, squeezed between China and Vietnam. If it had retained the 1995 level, it would have shared the 26th place with Belgium.

The publication of the index for 1997 had been big news for weeks in Buenos Aires; it had come at a time when Menem was trying to bend the constitutional rule that established that he could not run for president a third time. That year's index led to sharp complaints by the government against the Argentine Chapter of Transparency International, which had collected the survey data. Carlos Corach, the minister of the interior, stated that the index "conveys a lie, is unjust and absurd," adding that President Menem had mounted "the most formidable campaign to eradicate structural corruption." Mr. Jorge Rodríquez, Menem's chief of cabinet, had called the representative of TI for an explanation. This development helps explain the government's strong reaction to my paper. The concern that the IMF agreed with TI was a major one for the government.

The other development was that, at about the time when my paper was issued, the Fund was considering or, more likely, was being convinced by the Argentine authorities, to invite President Menem to the forthcoming Annual Fund-Bank Meetings, which would take place in Washington in late September. Menem would share the podium with Mr. Camdessus, the managing director of the IMF. This was an extraordinary honor rarely granted to a country. In general, the meetings were attended by the ministers of finance, central bank governors and their entourage. The only head of government that addressed the meeting, in the years it took place in Washington, was the president of the host country, the United States. Menem's attendance was being contemplated at a time when the talk of corruption concerning his administration was reaching a crescendo, and when there were enough concerns about economic developments that the deputy director of the IMF's Western Hemisphere Department, Mrs. Ter-Minassian, was reported to have warned the Argentine authorities that the country contained "a sort of Molotov cocktail" that could explode leading to a "speculative attack. This was reported by Paul Blustein in his book *And the Money Kept Rolling In (and Out)* (New York: Public Affairs, 2004; 54).

If Menem's invitation was surprising, the comments that the managing director of the IMF would make on October 1, 1998, at the press conference held at the end of the meetings, were even more surprising. He would refer to the Argentine experience in recent years as "exemplary" and remark that "Argentina had a story to tell the world: a story about the importance of fiscal discipline, of structural change, and of monetary policy rigorously maintained." For a country that, a few months earlier, had contained "a sort of Molotov cocktail," this was an extraordinary statement. It reflected a total lack of coordination between the office of the managing director, the department that dealt with Argentina on a daily basis, and the department charged with fiscal matters. The quote is taken from page 19 of the "Report on the Evaluation of the Role of the IMF in Argentina, 1991–2001" prepared by the Independent Evaluation Office of the IMF in June 30, 2004. It is difficult to understand where Mr. Camdessus was getting the information on which he based his comments.

President Menem had the honor of speaking at the IMF-World Bank Annual Meetings at a time when the economy was quickly entering a recession, the country risk was going sharply up (in part because of the Russian crisis), and Brazil was about to devalue, creating additional problems for Argentina. Clearly, the timing for Mr. Camdessus' remarks could not have been more unfortunate. However, it was consistent with the fact that, in 1998, the IMF had entered into an arrangement—called an Extended Fund Facility—that made large sums of money available to Argentina, with the understanding that the money would be used in case of necessity. The precautionary program was justified on the grounds that it would prevent the South East Asian and Russian crisis from spreading to Argentina and Latin America. If the problem had only been one of liquidity, this policy on the part of the IMF would have been the right one. Especially in 1998–1999, public spending would grow very fast to promote Menem's campaign for the third term. But, by this time, it should have been clear that the problem was not one of liquidity but one of public spending being consistently above available, ordinary resources. The difference was covered by foreign, and progressively more expensive loans. The year 1999 would bring a sharp recession and a further deterioration of the fiscal situation.

On October 29, 1999, I was invited back to Argentina by the IDEA, an institution that included some of the country's leading industrialists and public figures. I was invited to speak at the annual conference of IDEA to be held in Mar del Plata on November 4. Maria had joined me and we had made plans to go to Patagonia for a few days, because she had not been there and had heard so much about it from me. It would be my second trip to the south of Argentina; the first rapid one in 1994 had whetted my appetite. A few days before the conference, Fernando de la Rúa had won the elections against the candidate of the Justicialista (i.e. Peronist) party, Eduardo Duhalde. Menem had been legally prevented from running again.

I was flying to Buenos Aires from Rome, while Maria was coming from Washington. My plane was supposed to arrive at 6:00 a.m. and Maria's at 9:00 a.m., which made me wonder whether I should wait for her at the airport after a long overnight flight, or at the hotel. We agreed to meet at the airport; however, the problem was solved by the late arrival of my plane. I had almost missed the flight because there was an accident on the road to the airport in Rome and the traffic was stopped for a long while. This drove home to me the need for contingency plans. My wife did not have any idea of what to do when she arrived in Buenos Aires, apart from waiting for me at the airport and, at the time, there were still no cellular phones available to us. I had even forgotten to tell her in which hotel we were staying. In any case, we both arrived around 9:00 a.m., met and left for the hotel together. After checking in, we walked to Calle Florida and, from there, to Calle Lavalle, a street with many restaurants. I wanted to take Maria to a traditional and very Argentine steak house—La Estancia. There we had the usual fantastic beef; I had "bife de chorizo" and Maria had "bife La Estancia," which was twice the size of mine and must have weighed two pounds. I always wondered whether Argentines have more heart problems than citizens of other countries because of the quantity of red meat they consume per capita. If red meat is the culprit, it should show immediately in the statistics on cardiovascular disease.

The next morning we woke up at 4:00 a.m. to go to Patagonia. We went to Aeroparque Newbery, the domestic airport, which is conveniently located in the center of the city, along the River Plate. In terms of accessibility, it is even more convenient than Reagan National Airport in Washington. We checked in and got on the plane, which left punctually at 6:00 a.m. The flight to Río Gallegos took three full hours going straight south. Río Gallegos is one of the most southern cities in the world. It is a relatively small town but it is the capital of the province of Santa Cruz.

The flight was smooth. I read a bit, had breakfast, and slept a little. Upon arrival, we were met by a driver who took us to our hotel, about 400 km away! This time, the hotel was right in front of the Perito Moreno glacier. Patagonia is the size of California and Washington states, or say France and Spain, combined. It encompasses a huge area. The density of the population is very low, one person for every two square kilometers. Thus, it is essentially empty.

On the way we drove through La Esperanza (population about 10, but mentioned on the Atlas) and by Calafate (population 3,000–4,000). From Río Gallegos, the road to Perito Moreno is north-west. We finally arrived at the Hostería Los Notros, a charming small hotel with twenty rooms and a fantastic view of the glacier. The hotel had modern conveniences including telephone, fax, and e-mail, but these were not available in the rooms. Their e-mail address was LosNotros@Lastland.com. A very appropriate name!

We were received by three nice young ladies, and had lunch—meat, of course. Because my last medical check-up had indicated that my cholesterol level had gone up, this was not very good. On the other hand, the meat was delicious and we would try to eat less, hopefully! Because of our lack of choice, here we could indulge without feeling guilty.

At 4:00 p.m. a little bus from the hotel, driven by a young man from Spain, took us to an observation point just in front of the area where the glacier had touched the other side of the lake, cutting Lake Argentino into two parts. Since 1994, the previous time I had been here, the glacier had advanced all the way to the other side of the lake and the two parts could communicate only by tunnels through the glacier. These tunnels weakened the ice on top so big chunks of ice kept falling in the lake with thunderous sounds. To say that the glacier, which rises 200–300 feet above the level of the lake, is an incredible sight is a grand understatement. It is difficult to imagine the scene: high mountains all around with glaciers on top. The immense glacier that is Perito Moreno has a surface of high and uneven spikes that gives it a strange look. I had always thought that glaciers were smooth on top but this one was far from it. It had high towers and deep valleys. The reflections of the sun gave a bluish or almost turquoise look to the ice. The front of the glacier was a wall of ice. Many tunnels and grottos could be seen under the walls. A sign mentioned that forty people had been killed over the years when the falling ice created sharp projectiles that were thrown long distances in various directions and, like spears, had hit people. The observatory, built from wood, allowed one to gaze at the front of the glacier at a relatively close but safe proximity, and from different levels and angles. Signs advised visitors to stay on the observatories.

Although this was the second time that I saw this scene, I was awestruck. It was nature in its most pristine, beautiful and frightening best. There is really nothing I can think of that compares to it. When in 1994 Domingo Cavallo first told me about it, saying that it was the eighth wonder of the world, I thought it was the typical Argentine exaggeration. But he had not exaggerated, the place was just awesome. As we walked on the platform, a sign informed the visitors that camping at night was not allowed because there were pumas in the area. I must confess that I felt a bit uncomfortable and started looking around. Becoming food for a wild beast was not the end to my existence that I had contemplated.

We returned to the hotel after a couple of hours and sat on the terrace overlooking the glacier, which was about 5 km away. The name of the *hostería*—Los Notros—comes from a Patagonian red flower that, at this time, was in full bloom. The temperature was pleasant, especially when the sun was shining which, there, at that time of the year, it does until well past 8:00 p.m.

That evening, we had a good dinner of Patagonian trout, for a change, and a delicious dessert of crème caramel. The owners of the *hostería* had French names, which guaranteed that the food would be good—the French don't joke about their food! The next morning we woke up, took a shower, and had breakfast at 7:45. Then, we left the hotel by minibus to go to Puerto Bandera, about 50 km away. The bus was full of Italian-speaking tourists from either the north of Italy or Lugano in Switzerland; I could not tell which. At Puerto Bandera, on Lake Argentino, we boarded a large catamaran full of tourists. The catamaran would take us to see some other glaciers.

The first destination was the Upsala glacier, which is 60 km (37 miles) long, 10 km (4 miles) wide, and 60–80 m (200–250 ft) tall. With a surface of about 600 square kilometers, it is the largest glacier in South America. As the boat made its way toward the glacier, the chunks of ice in the water increased in number and became progressively larger. It took the boat one hour and a half to get as close to Upsala as possible, which meant within 4 km. There were several icebergs in the lake so the boat had to maneuver carefully around them. From time to time, my thoughts went to the *Titanic*, although our boat was moving slowly. The scenery became progressively more beautiful and unreal. The ice in the water acquired large proportions and very unusual shapes; some of the ice sculptures were real works of art. The weather was absolutely beautiful—not a cloud in the sky and a comfortable temperature. The whole trip was a real treat, a dream. I had almost never enjoyed myself as much in one day, or been as interested in the world around me, as I did on that day.

After the trip to the Upsala glacier, we turned around and headed for another destination, Bahía Onelli. At Onelli, we got off the boat to visit a forest. Patagonian forests are somewhat unusual: the trees are different; many are dead and many have strange twisted forms. It is obvious that they have a hard time surviving in that cold, windy and dry environment. I enjoyed taking pictures of dead trees and ghostly-looking ones that seemed to reproduce human or animal faces. We walked to the other side of the forest, a 20 to 30-minute walk, and came to a small lake into which three different glaciers landed. This was another extraordinary sight. The glaciers dropped big pieces of ice into the lake and the small icebergs, in all kinds of shapes, reflected the rays of the sun. This lake was the beginning of a fairly large river that originated in the lake and was fed by the glaciers. It was one of the grandest and purest natural sights I had ever seen. I was really sorry when we had to leave. Back at the hotel, I thought that I had had one of the most beautiful and fulfilling days of my life.

The next day, we were woken up at 7:00 a.m. by a knock on the door. We got dressed and went for breakfast—nothing fancy but abundant food. At 9:00 a.m. we were driven to a little harbor, not far from the hotel, where we waited for a boat that came a few minutes later. The people at the hotel had prepared a lunch box for us because we would not be back until 4:00 p.m. and there would not be any food where we were going.

The boat left promptly for the small trip that would take us to the left side of the Perito Moreno glacier. Soon we arrived at a little beach made up of colorful stones that clearly showed the grinding they must have taken when they had to bear the weight of the glacier. This place gave us a nice view of this side of the glacier and the mountains behind it. We left our lunch boxes in a small cabin that also contained toilet facilities. The whole group of about thirty was divided into three sub-groups, and each one was assigned to a separate guide. The division was largely by language: Spanish, English and Italian. Because of my wife's preference, we chose the

English-speaking group. We crossed the beach and entered a forest with its typical Patagonian look of dead trees and eerie scenes. We walked minutes through the forest for about fifteen and finally stood in front of the glacier. It looked imposing; we could see its hills and valleys well.

Shortly after, we were given metal boots with spikes at the bottom. The boots were to be placed on top of our normal shoes. The guide explained that they would facilitate walking and climbing on the ice. Without them, it would be slippery and dangerous. After putting on the iron boots, we were given instructions on how to walk on a glacier, something that one is hardly prepared for. We were told to keep our feet spread out, about one foot from each other, and to climb straight up or straight down. And, especially, to watch our step!

We started our trek which would last about two hours. The guide was very good but he still did not completely alleviate my apprehension. I had thought that the main difficulty would be climbing or descending the rather steep ice hills and valleys, some of them tens of meters high or tens of meters deep. However, my major concern soon became a different one: the fear of falling into the crevasses or deep holes that were all over the place. The unfreezing of the glacier in the Patagonian spring was forming small streams of ice water, which fell into deep holes that went all the way down to the bottom of the glacier, some 70–80 meters down. Some of these holes were wide enough for a person to fall in. I was also concerned that the ice would just give up under my feet and take me to a permanent, frozen-burial at the bottom of the glacier. The guide assured me that the ice was very strong and that it could not break under our feet. He advised me to just stay away from crevasses and holes and assured me that, by following his advice, I would survive!

We kept climbing hills and descending into valleys. The whole environment was as unreal and beautiful as anything I had ever seen. The boots were very useful—they really helped one to stay firm on the ground. I took lots of pictures of deep holes, crevasses, ice caves, and, of course, the whole scenery. I could not believe that the fable-like world I had seen from the observatory in front of Perito Moreno was now all around me, and that I was standing right on top of it. The sun kept disappearing and reappearing from behind the hills, giving a continually different look to what our eyes saw. Maria was a bit amused by my apprehension but as awestruck by the scenery as I was. I am sure, though, that she was a bit wary too.

To show the depth of the holes, the guide would throw pieces of ice into them and wait until we heard the sound the ice made when it reached the bottom. I could not help but think of the accident suffered by the son of an Argentine friend of mine who was mountain climbing in the Andes and fell into one of these crevasses. His body was never found.

We walked and climbed for about two hours and admired the scenery around us from various positions. The weather was a bit cold and windy, but not uncomfortable. Upon our descent from the highest point, we came across a valley and a pleasant surprise: the guides had placed a small wooden table, carried who knows when, right in the middle of the glacier and prepared a drink for everyone in the group. It was a pleasant surprise and a nice gesture. After the drink we made our way back to the edge of the glacier, walked back through the forest, and returned to the cabin where we had left our lunch box. We enjoyed our lunch which we ate sitting on the bare rocks facing the glacier. The view was magnificent and I kept thinking that I had been physically in the middle of the fable-like scenery I was now facing. The steep wall of the glacier stood at some 70–80 meters above the level of the lake and chunks of ice kept falling from it, making the thunder-like noises we had grown accustomed to. Occasionally, the chunks of ice that fell were so large that they created waves in the lakes.

The boat came to pick us up and, before returning, took us as close to the front wall of the glacier as it was safe to, giving us another much appreciated close-up of the glacier.

The next day we would go back to Buenos Aires. We had been in a room without telephone, radio or television and had not seen a newspaper. But we had not missed any of that; in fact, we had loved our isolation from the problems of the world.

On November 2, the driver picked us up at 9:00 a.m. for the 400-kilometer ride to the airport in Río Gallegos. He drove at great speed with only a few cars on the road, though a lot more cars than five years earlier. We were told that the number of tourists to Calafate had reached about 60,000 per year, half from outside Argentina. Again, we stopped at La Esperanza. The little diner had been expanded and there were more customers now. The group of Italians, or Italian-speaking Swiss, we had seen earlier were also at the diner. We saw faces that we had seen in the previous two days. Civilization was slowly coming to Patagonia. I hoped that it would not change much the character of the place.

When we reached the airport, we were told that the plane would be about three hours late. We had lunch at the airport café and sat down for the long wait. I did not mind waiting that much because I could use the time to prepare for my talk at the IDEA Conference. The plane finally arrived and we flew back to Buenos Aires. We were met at the airport and taken to the Alvear Palace Hotel. We went to sleep relatively early.

The next morning, we went to the airport for the charter flight to Mar del Plata. The flight was smooth until close to arrival, when high winds made it a bit bumpy. We landed and checked in at the Sheraton, a large, comfortable hotel where the conference would take place.

That evening, there was a dinner for several hundred people during which Domingo Cavallo spoke. He gave a good speech implicitly criticizing the new economic team's preoccupation with the short-run fiscal deficit and emphasizing all that had been done in previous years. He was obviously proud of developments that had been praised by those who had seen Argentina as a good example of what policies consistent with the Washington Consensus could do. He saw himself as the originator and promoter of those policies in Argentina. The economic team chosen by de la Rúa had expressed concern about the increasing public debt and the fiscal deficit. Cavallo spoke about the virtue of the Convertibility Law and praised the smooth election in which his political group had received 10 percent of the votes. This would give him a significant political platform from which he could aspire to higher positions in the future. This was the first election in Argentine history in which a president (Menem) had fully completed his term and been succeeded by a president from a different party through a free, democratic process. It was a major political achievement for the country.

The next morning there was a panel chaired by José Luis Machinea, Roque Fernández and Ricardo López Murphy. López Murphy was a well-known Argentine economist who would become economy minister for a few days in early 2001, when he would try to promote a genuine correction to the deteriorating fiscal accounts. Roque Fernández was the outgoing economy minister, and José Luis Machinea would be the incoming economy minister when President de la Rúa took office. There was some disagreement on what the fiscal deficit would be in the year 2000. Roque Fernández defended his tenure and assured the audience that he was leaving no surprises for the new government. The 1996–1998 period had been one of growth and the final data for 1999, which would make it a year of recession, were not yet in. It can be said that Roque Fernández and his team had done as well as they could given the circumstances. He received a long applause from the participants, among which were many of Argentina's leading industrialists. Machinea, on the other hand, argued that the fiscal deficit was higher than the officially reported one, and that the economy was in worse shape than claimed. He sounded like the spoiler of the "fiesta," so his talk received less applause. The final data for 1999 would prove him right.

In the afternoon, I took part in a panel with Juan Llach, an able Argentine economist interested in social issues who had held ministerial rank in earlier years. The theme was social justice and public expenditure. In my presentation, I elaborated on the experience with the growth of public spending in developed countries and on the need to make public spending efficient. I emphasized that public spending in Argentina was neither low nor efficient. It required high tax levels to be fully financed. Over the 1990s, public spending had grown enormously in real terms and had always exceeded ordinary revenue in spite of the fast rate of growth and generally good and increasing real revenue. Given the apparent incapacity of the government to cut public spending, the only alternative would be to raise the level of taxation enough to cover the fiscal gap, hoping that this increase in revenue would not itself invite more spending. I outlined some changes in taxation that I would have liked to see in Argentina. I mentioned, especially, that I would have liked an increased reliance on the personal income tax, which was paid by only a few taxpayers and which generated hardly any revenue. I called attention to the persistence of the fiscal deficit and to the growth of public and, especially foreign, debt, and warned about the danger that this created for the Argentine economy. I stressed that a fiscal adjustment of only a couple of points of GDP, possibly obtained through an increase in the personal income tax on those who had benefited the most from the economic expansion of the 1990s, if sustained over time, would not be very painful and could prevent serious future problems. I concluded that, based on current trends, the country would sooner or later get into serious trouble.

My speech was widely reported by Argentine newspapers. I was surprised as it received more attention than those of most other speakers. The next morning I received several early phone calls from radio stations who wanted to interview me. I accepted the first three and then stopped answering the phone. Unfortunately, while my talk was receiving a lot of attention in Buenos Aires, it seemed to receive none in Washington. The managing director of the Fund had, jokingly, accused me of being a pessimist, to which I replied that, at times, a pessimist is just a realist with better information. Three months later, in March 2000, the IMF and Argentina would agree to a so-called Stand-by Arrangement (SBA) of $7.2 billion. The amount would be increased to $13.7 billion in January 2001 and to $22 billion in September 2001. In December 2001, the Fund would cut its support to Argentina and the country would default on $103 billion on its debt. It would be the biggest default in history.

The night of my presentation there was another large dinner. My wife and I were seated near the main table, where the president-elect, de la Rúa, was seated. Sitting at our table was the head of Fiat in Argentina, who complained about high taxes on enterprises and, especially, about the tax on gross assets, the minimum tax on enterprises, which in his view was unfair because it taxed enterprises that "never had any profits." The dinner speaker was President Fernando de la Rúa. He gave a forceful speech, but one lacking in details, on what the government wanted to do. He emphasized that the good aspects of the Menem administration—specifically the Convertibility Law—would be preserved, but the bad aspects would be changed. The bad aspects referred to issues of corruption and social justice. He came across as a sober, well-intentioned, and low-key individual. At the dinner, I also met de la Sota, the governor of the province of Córdoba. I had been his lunch guest in Córdoba, when I received the honorary degree from that university. My department had provided some technical assistance to his province.

We returned to Buenos Aires and took advantage of the day to walk around San Telmo, an area with antique shops, and La Recoleta, where we had a nice dinner with my former student, Armando, and his lady friend, Mónica. As usual, we ate fantastic Argentine beef. Later, I had a meeting with José Luis Machinea and Juan Carlos Gómez Sabaini to discuss, privately and confidentially, some ideas they had on tax reform. The objectives were to raise more revenue and to increase the equity of the tax system. We seemed to coincide on several desirable changes. That evening, we joined Carlos Silvani, the revenue secretary, at Casablanca, a tango place where Maria could enjoy exceptionally good tango before our return to Washington. Because of Carlos' presence, we got very good seats. Revenue secretaries and tax directors usually carry a lot of weight with important taxpayers so one is always guaranteed a good seat.

CHAPTER X

Argentina, the IMF, and the Default of 2001

During the year 2000, my last year at the IMF, I did not go back to Argentina but continued to follow a story of which, I was convinced, I knew the end. Some of my writing on fiscal deficits and on public debt had prepared me for it. During the decade of the 1990s, the long term dynamic disequilibrium in the fiscal accounts, created by a society that over the long run wanted a level of public spending larger than what it was prepared or able to finance (through taxes or other *ordinary* revenues), had been covered in different ways: First, by exceptional revenue sources and then, more and more, by foreign loans, a substantial part of which came from the IMF. IMF loans are expected to be repaid in a relatively short span. In the first half of the 1990s, the revenue from the 1989 tax reform, the "Tanzi effect" associated with the fall in inflation, the large proceeds from the privatization of public enterprises, and the higher real revenue coming from the very high growth rates of the economy in those years, had kept the fiscal deficit relatively low in spite of sharply rising real public spending.

But as time passed, especially after 1994, the exceptional revenue sources started to dry up and the government relied more and more on foreign loans. As the foreign debt rose and interest rates became progressively higher, because of Argentina's growing country risk or because of increasing risk aversion on the part of international creditors (due to financial crises, especially in 1995 and 1997–1998), an increasing share of total government revenue was required to service the public debt. This created a situation that could not continue for long, especially in an economy that was still relatively closed in its foreign trade. Exports as a share of GDP had risen from about 6 percent in 1992 to about 9 percent in 2000. The foreign debt was soon several times the size of Argentina's annual exports, raising the question of whether it could ever be repaid. This made the loans more expensive and of shorter maturity. The servicing of the foreign debt reduced the revenue available for domestic primary spending, particularly for the central government. Clearly, a Ponzi game was in effect. At some point, the foreign loans would, first, become very expensive and, later, dry up completely. That point could not be postponed forever.

Some economists, and especially those with a more macroeconomic bend, including Guillermo Calvo, an Argentine economist who, until the end of 2006, was the chief economist at the InterAmerican Development Bank, have blamed mainly foreign developments for the Argentine crisis of 2001–2002. Calvo has pointed out that the beginning of the 2000s was unfavorable for Argentina, because external factors had largely neutralized the positive effects associated with changes promoted by, or consistent with, the so-called Washington Consensus during the decade of the 1990s. He has given a lot of importance to the flow of international capital and to the international cost of borrowing. But, of course, the cost of borrowing for a specific country is a reflection of the world interest rate *and* of domestic factors. In Argentina, domestic factors became progressively more significant in the years before the debt default. While there is obviously some merit in Calvo's position, in my judgment it underestimates the corrosive impact that fiscal deficits, maintained over long periods, and especially if financed by external sources, can have on a country's economy.

The loans that Argentina got from the IMF over the 1990s were by far the cheapest source of credit that it could get. This created a strong incentive on the part of the Argentine authorities to continue pressuring the IMF for more financing. During my last year at the IMF, I became progressively more frustrated because the Fund was not able or willing to see what was happening in Argentina. It failed to realize that the financing it had been making available to that country was not being used to make essential structural reforms, as it was intended to, but it was financing politically motivated projects and was simply extending the day of reckoning, which would make the final outcome more costly for both Argentina and foreign creditors. I was not overly concerned about the lenders from Wall Street, who had made a lot of money out of Argentina over the years, but I began to worry about other lenders. I began to feel that, in case of default, the IMF would bear some responsibility toward those who were lending money to Argentina believing that, because of the Fund's presence, an economic adjustment was going on. These creditors were different from the large financial institutions, which were able to spread the risk and were aware of the risks they were taking. These institutions would be quicker in getting out at the first evident sign of danger thus minimizing their losses, but the non-institutional lenders did not have the benefit of good, private analyses.

By the year 2000, the Fund had so many billions tied up in Argentina that stopping the lending would have made the country go immediately into default. This would have created difficulties not only for Argentina but also for the IMF's financial accounts. This unwelcome outcome could be delayed by lending with one hand and having Argentina meet its financial obligations to the Fund with the other hand, while all the time waiting or hoping for a miracle. Argentina, together with Brazil and Turkey, was one of the major contributors to Fund income, the income that was paying my salary.

The danger of default was clouded by the ongoing academic discussion on whether the problem facing Argentina was one of "liquidity" or "solvency." This distinction, made by some economists with great precision and conviction, always seemed somewhat artificial to me. What is the meaning of solvency when the political or legal system of a country prevents the economic minister from correcting a growing imbalance? Can financing keep a country from going broke forever? In theory it can, if the lenders keep lending money and the country keeps servicing its debt through further borrowing, which is what had been happening in Argentina. But this is a Ponzi scheme that in the real world cannot continue forever.

The election of President de la Rúa introduced a new element to the situation. It created a complication that was frequent in Fund dealings with countries. This was the coming into the scene of a new administration and new policymakers that could not be blamed for *past* policies and mistakes. In theory, the Fund deals with countries, but in reality it deals with individuals and these change from time to time. The Menem administration, which, especially in later years, was responsible for the deterioration of the fiscal accounts, and which had often not delivered, or not delivered fully, on the promises for policy changes made to the Fund, was out. That administration had played the IMF card masterfully. Could the Fund penalize the new administration for the sins of the previous one? It did not seem fair. The government that took power in December 1999 seemed to represent a clear break from the past and was made up of serious individuals. How should the Fund react to this new opportunity? Shouldn't the new government be given the benefit of the doubt? In the end, the new government was given more than the benefit of the doubt. It was given a new credit card with a potentially *very* large balance on it. The question that remained unanswered was whether this government would have the power and the determination to correct permanently the fiscal imbalance and make other essential reforms. It would soon become obvious that it would not have the power.

In March 2000, the Board of the Fund approved a "stand-by arrangement," that is a line of credit available to the Argentine government, provided that it satisfied particular conditions stipulated in the agreement. Once again, large financing was being provided in exchange for promises. The amount of the loan was very large by any standards. The assumption was that the size of the loan would give assurance to the market so private credit would continue to be available to the country at reasonable rates. The underlying belief was that the *mood of the market, and not the fiscal disequilibrium and the large and growing debt, were the main problems.* The view was: "keep Wall Street happy and the money will continue flowing in." Once again, the problem was seen as one of liquidity and not of the capacity to change direction. However, the loan could not do anything about solving the dynamic long-term fiscal disequilibrium problem that was getting worse. It could only postpone the day of reckoning.

Apart from the initial sizeable disbursement that accompanied the signing of the agreement, the money would be disbursed to the Argentine government over a three-year period, as long as it carried out the agreed reforms. Periodic program reviews would establish if this had occurred and occasional waivers for non-compliance with some of the promises made to the Fund would be discussed and approved by the IMF's Board. Part of the loans would, once again, be used to repay to the Fund and to other creditors the loans that were reaching maturity. This would preserve the appearance that there was no arrears with the IMF or with other creditors. The Fund's accounts would continue to show a healthy income. If normal accounting standards had been used, as applied to commercial banks, which make a distinction between performing and bad loans, it is not clear how these loans would have been classified in the accounts of the IMF. However, for the time being, they provided an apparently healthy income to the Fund.

Unfortunately, the de la Rúa administration would soon run into old problems and face some new ones. The first problem was the strong reaction by the labor unions to the labor reform pushed by the government and approved in April 2000 by the Argentine Senate, and in May, by the Lower House of Parliament. This was one of two reforms that the IMF had been urging for years. This reform aimed at making the labor market more flexible and the country more competitive. The other reform concerned the fiscal arrangements with the provincial governments. The latter had continued to share in the revenues of *national* taxes and to overspend, making the control of the fiscal accounts of the whole public sector very difficult. Each time the national government attempted to raise taxes to reduce the fiscal deficit, about half of the total tax increase went to the provincial governments, which immediately spent all the additional income and often more. National strikes were called by the powerful labor unions creating political turbulence and uncertainty about the future.

The approval of the labor reform created great political difficulties for the administration, and it was accused of having bought the approval on the Senate by the payment of bribes to some senators. For an administration that had been elected partly because it was believed to be clean and, for this reason, had been compared favorably to the previous administration, this was not a good development. A consequence of it was the resignation, sometime later, of the vice president, Carlos Álvarez, bringing considerable disarray to the new team and the loss of part of the political forces that had helped the de la Rúa administration win the election. De la Rúa badly needed the support of these forces. The Corruption Perception Index (CPI) of Transparency International (TI), which had improved significantly in 2000, would soon head south and would reach, once again, very low levels in future years. In special surveys conducted in 2003 and 2004 by Gallup International for Transparency International, "political parties" got the worst (i.e., most corrupted) score in Argentina than in any of the countries surveyed (47 countries in 2003 and 62 countries in 2004). "Parliament/Legislature" also got the lowest score among the countries in Argentina.

A second problem was the perennial, but fast worsening, fiscal problem. The economy minister, José Luis Machinea, was well-intentioned and determined to contain the fiscal deficit and the growth of the public debt, and he had taken some significant early steps in that direction. However, the weakening state of the economy and the increasing levels of the interest rates that raised the costs of *refinancing* the now fast maturing debt, made it difficult for him to succeed. At that time, a lot of past debt was reaching maturity and, even if new financing had been available, it would be available at sharply increasing interest rates.

In 2000, due to the effort of the new administration, tax revenue increased by about 0.5 percent of GDP and *primary* spending (that is spending net of interest payments) was maintained at the previous year's level. Thus, the fiscal accounts should have improved. In fact, they improved in terms of the *primary balance*, a fact that seemed to impress some observers who feel, wrongly, that all a country has to worry about is the primary balance, that is, the fiscal balance before interest payments. However, the interest paid on the foreign debt went up by more than 1 percent of GDP. It would go up by another 1 percent of GDP in 2001. Clearly an unsustainable debt dynamic had been set in motion.

In numerous newspaper articles, some economists, and especially Joseph Stiglitz in his book *Globalization and Its Discontents* (Norton, 2002 and 2003), have criticized the IMF for pushing countries to try to contain the growth of fiscal deficits during financial crises. Thus, they have criticized the fiscal actions of the Argentine government in trying to contain the growth of the fiscal deficit in 2000 and 2001. They have also criticized the IMF for removing the financial support that it had provided Argentina over the years. As Stiglitz put it in his book: "For more than seventy years there has been a standard recipe for a country facing a severe economic downturn. The government must stimulate aggregate demand, either by monetary or fiscal policy—cut taxes, increase expenditures, or loosen monetary policy" (page 105 of the 2003 edition). That is, the government should push the central bank to print more money or it should cut taxes and spend more. This criticism has been echoed by reporters and, in Argentina, especially by Ernesto Tenembaum in his bestselling book on Argentina and the IMF, *Enemigos* (Grupo Editorial Norma, 2004).

These criticisms are perplexing. It is difficult for me to understand how a country can finance a fiscal stimulation of aggregate demand when it has to borrow *abroad* the money to finance that expansion and when the interest rate at which it can borrow has become very high and would become even higher if the deficit became larger and the country tried to borrow more. In Argentina, by the year 2001, the growth of external public debt and the rise in interest rates on that debt had created a clearly explosive situation. The interest payment on that debt had been 1.10 percent of GDP in 1993; had risen to 1.94 percent of GDP in 1997; and had jumped to 3.92 percent of GDP in 2000, and to 4.80 percent of GDP in 2001, when it was absorbing about one fourth of total tax revenue and almost

50 percent of exports earnings. If the government had attempted to stimulate aggregate demand by borrowing even more, interest payments would have increased further, sharply absorbing the additional borrowing and thus neutralizing the expansionary impact of the fiscal deficit because the interest payments were made abroad. The Convertibility Law, which had tied the peso to the dollar, and the historical experience with inflationary finance, which had led to that law, had closed the possibility of a monetary expansion.

Critics, even those with a Nobel Prize in economics, may not realize, or may fail to acknowledge, that a fiscal deficit has to be financed somehow. For you to be able to spend more than your income, you need someone to give you credit. Governments, just like individuals, cannot ignore this aspect. Without financing, there cannot be a fiscal deficit. Or, more often, if there is no *additional* financing, there cannot be a *larger* fiscal deficit. In many circumstances, there is a limit to the size of the fiscal deficit that a country can have. I have explained this in a paper published and buried in a conference volume in 1984. The paper, "Is There a Limit to the Size of Fiscal Deficits in Developing Countries?" was published in *Public Finance and Public Debt*, edited by Bernard P. Herber, *Proceedings of the 40th Congress of the International Institute of Public Finance* (Wayne State University Press). Unfortunately, conference volumes tend to be like black holes for the papers that they contain because few read these volumes. This paper had not attracted any attention.

When a government can no longer borrow from the central bank either because the laws of the country prevent it from doing so; or because the borrowing has created high inflation, with the accompanying reduction in tax revenue (as reported in Chapter III), the only source of financing is the sale of bonds to the public. If the bonds can easily be sold domestically, *at unchanging or little changing interest rates*, then pursuing a fiscal expansion, at least in the short run, may not create economic difficulties. This happens routinely in advanced countries under normal circumstances; it is the situation contemplated by Stiglitz. In these countries, recessions may even bring *reductions* in interest rates, because borrowing for private investment falls. However, if the bonds cannot be sold domestically, and the central bank is not allowed to, or cannot print money, the only source of financing is loans from abroad, in addition to less orthodox and limited possibilities such as raiding the accounts of social security institutions or not paying salaries or suppliers. The loans become, first, progressively more expensive, thus leading to increases in the deficit and in the payments made to foreigners; and then they vanish. This would happen in Argentina in late 2001. It would have happened much earlier without the IMF's loans and programs. In conclusion, a government with its fiscal accounts already in bad shape, which can only borrow abroad at exorbitant and increasing rates, can hardly afford to pursue an expansionary fiscal policy as recommended by Stiglitz, Tenembaum, and others. I am sure that de la Rúa and Machinea would have been happy to follow Stiglitz' advice if it had been possible to do so.

Actually, the top management of the IMF may have been much closer to Stiglitz' view than it is realized. One of Argentina's best informed economists, Mario Teijeiro, himself a former Fund employee, pointed out in one of his articles written in 2002 that, as late as October 2000, Stanley Fischer, then the first deputy managing director at the IMF, still maintained that Argentina's first priority was economic growth and not fiscal adjustment. In his view, with growth the fiscal problem would solve itself. Teijeiro reports that, at that time (October 2000), Fischer had declared that the correct policy for Argentina was to "increase its fiscal deficit through a tax reduction." This would promote growth. Teijeiro reports that, by June 2001, Fischer had changed his view and that, at that time, he had advised the Argentine authorities to persevere with the fiscal adjustments that the authorities were attempting to make. Teijeiro accuses the Fund of having become totally permeable to the interests of the international lenders. Teijeiro's article is titled "Los Consejos de Stanley Fischer" (The recommendations of Stanley Fischer).

A third problem may have been de la Rúa's personality. While Menem had been perceived as street smart, perhaps not very principled, but decisive; de la Rúa was soon seen as a nice and decent guy who lacked the managerial and tough personality essential in the situation Argentina found itself in at the time. De la Rúa would have been a good leader in normal circumstances, but he was not the right person to lead Argentina in 2000 and 2001. Stories started circulating that at meetings with his cabinet ministers would not show up on time and De la Rúa, who was always punctual, occasionally had to wait, at times practically by himself, for the others to arrive in order to start cabinet meetings. Somehow, it is difficult to think that this would have happened with Menem. Jokes started circulating about the fact that de la Rua's main identifying trait was his lack of ideas on how to solve problems. Fairly or unfairly, these descriptions reduced his status and his political clout making it more and more difficult for him and for his ministers to promote the necessary changes.

In October 2000, when I was practically out of the IMF and in the process of joining Carnegie Endowment for International Peace (CEIP), a Washington think-tank, as a senior associate, I was invited by Nancy Birdsall to attend a meeting with Latin American leaders. Dr. Birdsall was a former World Bank economist who, for a while, had been vice president of the InterAmerican Development Bank and, at that time, was also a senior associate at CEIP. The meeting took place outside New York City, at one of the Rockefeller family's mansions. By this time, the de la Rúa administration was in serious difficulties and the interest rate at which Argentina could get foreign credit had gone through the roof, with the country risk at around 900 basis points. Thus, it cost the Argentine government about 9 percent more than the U.S. Treasury to borrow money. Machinea was having serious difficulties in preventing the public finances from getting completely out of hand, and the Argentine administration was pushing the IMF for still more (or better, much more) money. Domingo Cavallo was one of the Latin American leaders attending the meeting. At that time, he was not part of the Argentine government but he must have sensed that he would soon play a major role in it. After Machinea's resignation, on March 2, 2001, and a brief interlude with Ricardo López Murphy as economy minister, in which he tried unsuccessfully to sharply cut public spending, Cavallo would join the de la Rúa administration as economy minister (on March 20, 2001).

At the meeting at the Rockefeller mansion, Cavallo forcefully defended the Convertibility Law hinting, however, that some minor changes in the law might be necessary. These changes involved giving some weight to the euro, which had become a new major currency. During breaks from the formal part of the meeting, he asked my opinion on some fiscal changes that were being discussed in Buenos Aires. One was the replacement of the value-added tax with a retail sales tax imposed at the point when purchases are made by final consumers. Apparently, this idea was attracting some following in Buenos Aires. The other was the privatization of the tax revenue collection, essentially closing down the Dirección General Impositiva (the tax office) and assigning the responsibility to a private group or groups. Listening to Cavallo, I could not fail to recall the various magical solutions to the fiscal problems that I had heard over the decades.

As for the first idea, I explained to him that concentrating the whole tax liability on the last step (at the retail sale) was too dangerous because it would stimulate tax evasion. I reminded him that a large part of the revenue from the value-added tax (often as much as half) is collected at the import stage. The self-enforcing mechanism of the value-added tax, which often guarantees that the government gets at least some revenue, would be lost. I explained that no country in the world had ever imposed or maintained a retail sales tax with a rate higher than 10 percent and that, even 10 percent, had proven too high in countries with good tax compliance. At a 10 percent rate, collected only at the retail stage, given the probable productivity of that tax in Argentina, the revenue collected would be not more than half of what Argentina was collecting at that time from the value-added tax. Thus, the country could lose as much as 3 percent of GDP in revenue. Argentina was hardly in a condition to run this risk.

Interestingly, in 2005 a similar idea was being pushed in the United States by a book that briefly made the bestseller list. The idea was to replace *all* the taxes collected by the Internal Revenue Service with a single retail sales tax applied with a rate of 23 percent. The authors of this book argued that, in the process, the IRS could be abolished because it would no longer be needed. See *The Fair Tax Book* by Neal Boortz (a talk show host) and Congressman John Linder (Regan Books, 2005). I could not help but think that this book should have been called *The Fairy Tale Tax Book*. This was essentially the idea mentioned by Cavallo five years earlier, but extended to the whole U.S. tax system. Of course the U.S. does not have a value added tax, so the tax would replace income and excise taxes. This indicates that strange or impractical tax ideas do not originate only in Argentina; and when they do, they are exported to other places. In 2007, a bill was presented to the U.S. Congress by John Linder proposing the change.

As to the idea of privatizing the collection of taxes, I strongly argued against it. I explained to Cavallo that the main problem with tax administration was not collection, which could easily be and was often done through banks, but the difficulties in auditing, settling litigations, and enforcing compliance. These functions could not be privatized. I had often been in favor of privatization, but this was one privatization carried a bit too far. Apart from its intrinsic merit, or more likely demerit, the change itself would be so unsettling that it would create chaos, at least during the transition phase, in an already chaotic fiscal situation.

I was happy to see that when Cavallo became minister three months later, these ideas were not pursued, even though the instinct to experiment with unorthodox tax changes, rather than focusing on strengthening traditional taxes, did not abandon him. By this time, Carlos Silvani, the revenue secretary, had resigned in protest over the introduction of a tax amnesty that had been announced before being introduced and that may have contributed to the fall in tax compliance in early 2001. Like devaluations, tax amnesties cannot be discussed publicly before they are enacted. It is also an open question whether they should ever be enacted.

At the end of November 2000, I left the IMF and joined Carnegie Endowment for International Peace. A short time after my retirement from the Fund, I was interviewed by *La Nación* which, in the section *Economía y Negocios* of December 17, 2000, dedicated two full pages to the interview titled "La Argentina recauda como Haití y gasta como Europa" (Argentina taxes like Haiti and spends like Europe). I repeated some of my earlier criticisms of Argentine economic policy and my concern about the situation. I also expressed my disagreement with some of the policies that had been promoted by the IMF.

I spent the month of March 2001 as a visiting professor at the University of Munich in Germany and, in May 2001, I was invited to join the government of Silvio Berlusconi, who had just won the Italian election. I was offered the position of undersecretary for economy and finance so I moved from Washington to Rome and was largely cut off from the IMF and from Argentina. However, given my past interest in the country and the dramatic developments that affected it in 2001, developments that would have a big impact on Italian savers, I continued to follow the news about Argentina mainly through newspapers. During the following months, I had some contacts with the Argentine Embassy in Rome and was forced to pay attention to Argentina in connection with different episodes that I will describe briefly.

In the late summer of 2001, I received a call from the Argentine ambassador to Italy, Mrs. Elsa Kelly, telling me that Domingo Cavallo, who in March 2001 had become Argentina's new minister of economy, was coming to Rome for a visit and wanted to meet with the Italian minister of economy and finance, Giulio Tremonti. Could I help arrange a meeting? By this time, the Argentine economy was often on the front page of newspapers and it was likely that Cavallo was visiting Europe in a desperate search for loans. The spread between what the Argentine government had to pay to get loans from the financial market and what the U.S. Treasury had to pay was, by this time, approaching 2000 basis points. Argentina was reaching the point when it would be cut out completely from access to the financial market, regardless of the interest rate it was willing to pay. I tried to arrange the meeting but Tremonti declared that he would not be available. He suggested that *I* receive Cavallo. Obviously this would not be the same thing because Tremonti had the political power that would have been necessary to provide loans from Italy to Argentina; I did not have such power. In any case, given the deteriorating fiscal situation of Italy at the time, and the increasingly strident public debate about it, it would have been very difficult to engineer a loan. What Italy could do was support the new loan that the IMF was contemplating, which would be approved on September 7, 2001.

The ambassador decided that, instead of Cavallo coming to see me at the ministry, a luncheon would be arranged at the embassy. I was not told whether this reflected the view of the embassy or a preference by Cavallo. I was then asked to suggest the names of high level individuals who could be invited to the luncheon. I suggested the governor of the Bank of Italy, some ministers interested in, or with some background in, economics, and high level individuals in Parliament and in the financial market. A short time later, I got a rather desperate call from Ambassador Kelly telling me that on one on the list was available. I was somewhat annoyed because I thought that the prominence of Cavallo and the importance of Argentina merited more attention. But, obviously, the Argentine financial difficulties were making people nervous; or perhaps the non-availability of these individuals was simply due to the fact that it was summer and that Italians take their summer vacation seriously. Finally, the luncheon turned out to be a small affair with Cavallo, Ambassador Kelly, Professors Luigi Spaventa and Antonio Pedone, both from the University of Rome and both with considerable political background, myself, and a couple of other people from the embassy. It was a somewhat melancholic lunch during which I could not help but feel sorry for Cavallo and consider the mission to which he had volunteered as the closest thing to a "mission impossible." Obviously, he must have felt that he would be able to make a difference through his presence in the government, but the economic storm that was moving toward Argentina was much too strong and much too close for anyone to stop it at this time.

In his desperate attempt to deal with the approaching financial crisis, Cavallo tried to gain extra time by negotiating with New York bankers a lengthening of the maturity of some loans. By this time, the major problem was how to refinance the huge loans that were reaching maturity and not to just finance the fiscal deficit. This arrangement inevitably cost Argentina tens of millions of dollars but had little or no effect on the real problem. The menacing clouds would soon be over Buenos Aires and Argentina would no longer be able to service the maturing debt obligations. Neither Cavallo's energy, dexterity, and imagination, nor the IMF's financial support, would be sufficient to prevent the imminent default.

As the end of 2001 approached, the storm was fully over Buenos Aires. There were riots against the government and President de la Rúa and his administration resigned. In a desperate attempt to keep the fiscal accounts under some control, the financial assets of the pension system were raided. This was the only source of financing the fiscal deficit left to the government. The pension system was forced to buy public bonds, while at the same time, the savings of Argentines had been locked in the banks.

The so-called "corralito," imposed in December 2001, was the last act of the de La Rúa administration. It started as a form of capital controls to limit the amount of cash withdrawals from banks, at a time when the country was undergoing a complicated debt restructuring process aimed at trying to prevent default, and when pesos could still be converted into dollars at the rate of one to one. In this original version, it did not actually freeze bank accounts because, during the "corralito," people could still use the money in the accounts to do purchases as long as they used checks or credit cards; but they could not withdraw cash. Obviously, not all Argentines had credit cards or checking accounts. The actual "freezing" of the bank accounts took place in January 2002, when the Duhalde administration, then in power, converted the "corralito" into the so-called "corralón." Duhalde's "corralón" froze bank accounts after his administration decided to forcibly convert the currency denomination of dollar deposits into pesos (the so-called "pesoification"). The Argentine population would suffer huge losses as they were ripped off of their savings. This would lead to a rapid and large increase in the poverty line.

On December 23, 2001, the new president, Adolfo Rodriguez Sáa, announced default on Argentina's external debt. His declaration would be welcomed by applause in the Argentine Congress. This would be the largest default in history; affecting $103 billions in foreign loans. The default did not apply to the official debt toward international financial institutions, but only to the debt toward private creditors. On January 6, 2002 the Convertibility Law was abolished and the peso was allowed to depreciate freely. By March 25, 2002, the peso had reached a level of four to the dollar, from the parity (one to one) it had held until January 6. This made the many Argentine citizens who had large assets abroad much richer in terms of Argentine pesos, and the much greater number of Argentines with assets in Argentine banks much poorer as their assets had been converted into pesos at the rate of one to one before the devaluation. It also sharply reduced the real debt of enterprises, which could now repay it at the much cheaper pesos instead of dollars. In the following four years the peso would recover some of the lost value before inflation became a concern again. The large devaluation would promote exports, and the "pesoification" would make many enterprises profitable once again. This stimulus would accompany the international commodity boom of recent years, giving Argentina once again a good period for several years after the crisis. This period allowed it to recover the lost output.

In February 2002, I was invited to be part of an international group of "wise men," created to advise the new Argentine administration on possible steps to take in relation to the foreign debt and the accounts of Argentine citizens that were frozen in Argentine banks. The group, made up of about ten members, represented various countries and especially countries that had lent money to Argentina. I represented Italy. The group was invited to a meeting in Buenos Aires, where I would be a guest at the residence of the Italian ambassador, Mr. Nígido, an able and pleasant diplomat. The group met for a full day, first with the minister and then with the technical staff of the ministry of economy. There was a lot of discussion but, not surprisingly, no solution was found to the Argentine economic mess. Everyone agreed that it was a mess so, in some sense, there was some agreement among the group. I stressed the need to look at the link between the fiscal developments and the crisis. After this meeting, the committee of "wise men" died a natural death; it was never reconvened. The Argentine experts must have concluded that the "wise men" were not wise enough to solve their problems.

At this time, the extent of the sharp rise in Argentina's poverty was becoming known. A large portion of the population had quickly made the transition from being part of the middle class to being poor. As it happened in Korea in 1978, in the middle of the financial crisis of Southeast Asia, newspapers were full of stories about individuals and families who, from one day to the next, had become poor. In Italy there were attempts, in part coordinated by the Roman municipal administration, to collect non-perishable food to send to the Argentine poor. As an economist, I could not fail to consider this a strange development. The idea of sending food all the way from Italy to Argentina, one of the richest agricultural countries in the world, and one which had historically exported large quantities of food products to the world, was peculiar. For sure, it would have been far more efficient to send money, as the Nobel Prize winner in economics, Amartya Sen, had argued in his study of famines in India. In these situations, money is always far more effective than specific goods, including food.

While in Rome, one of my responsibilities was to represent the ministry of economy and finance in some of the committees in the Italian Parliament, during meetings that discussed proposed legislation with economic implications. One day, a member of Parliament approached me and asked if I would be wiling to meet with an individual from his jurisdiction who needed some advice regarding Argentina. I agreed and we made arrangements for this individual to come to see me at the ministry.

A well-dressed, middle-aged gentleman came to my office and told me a story that I found very interesting. Apparently, he had an uncle who had emigrated to North America many years before and had rarely been in touch with his relatives in Italy, including his sister who was the mother of the individual in my office. Recently, the uncle had died and had left the nephew some property in Italy. He had also left some documents that gave access to a safety box in a country in the Americas (not Argentina) and a key to the box. Assuming that the box might contain something of value, my visitor had traveled to the foreign country and had opened the box. To his surprise, the box was very large and contained a huge quantity of money in one million bills issued by Argentina's Central Bank. To be precise, there were 40 billion pesos in the box! The origin of this money was a mystery to my visitor because, as far as he knew, his uncle had never lived in Argentina and he had never learned what activities his uncle had been engaged in.

Thinking that he had inherited a huge fortune that would make him one of Italy's richest men, he had transported, at considerable expense, the content of the box to a Swiss safe deposit. However, he still had no idea about the current value of this treasure so he asked me if I could help him determine just how rich he was. I contacted my former colleague at the Fund, Mario Blejer, who at that time was vice president of Argentina's Central Bank, and discovered that the particular bills, issued in 1980, were no longer in circulation. They had been withdrawn a long time ago. Furthermore, even if they still had legal status, the inflation since 1980 would have dramatically reduced their present real value.

I asked my wife, a statistician and a staff member of the Statistics Department of the IMF, if she could determine the current value of 40 billion in 1980 pesos. When she gave me the results a few days later, I was astonished. The present value of the 40 billion pesos from 1980 had been reduced over the years to about 1 U.S. dollars. This reminded me of the fact that the rule of compounding had always impressed Einstein. It also reminded me of an article published in the *New York Times* on July 25, 1993, which dealt with Brazil, a country that had also experienced high inflation. As the article had put it: "Since 1980 . . . without the currency changes, a cup of coffee that sold in 1980 for 15 cruzeiros would sell today for 22 billion cruzeiors." I was also reminded of IMF missions to Bolivia in the 1980s, when members of the missions had to go around with large handbags carrying the money to pay for lunches or dinners.

I informed the gentleman who, of course, could not believe the estimate. He had invested a large amount of his money in what he thought was an enterprise that would make him one of Italy's richest men. In an indirect and presumably unintentional way, his uncle had played a cruel joke on him. This story gave me a very graphic illustration of what had happened in Argentina since 1980. I did not see the gentleman again and never learned the end of the story.

Another development was more emotionally draining for me because it tested my loyalty toward the institution I had worked for during twenty-seven years (the IMF), and the country and government that I represented at that time. I soon became aware that the Argentine default could be a significant blow not only for the many Argentines who would lose their savings and would move into poverty, but also for some Italian savers who had bought Argentine bonds. In Italy, there had been retail purchase of Argentine bonds by individual investors. I learned that Italian savers had been buying Argentine bonds well into 2001, when the Argentine situation was moving toward chaos and when better informed Wall Street investors were pulling out. The Italian savers had been attracted by the high rates on Argentine bonds, compared with the low and falling rates on Italian bonds, and by the belief that only individuals can fail, not countries.

When I first learned about the Italian investments in Argentine bonds, I dismissed the problem because the three people I knew who had bought Argentine bonds were: the rich wife of an Italian minister, a former minister and former president of a large Italian bank, and a former president of a commission in Parliament. All three were smart enough, I thought, to have known what they were doing when they decided to buy Argentine bonds. At that time, I was not aware of the dimension of the problem for Italy. Soon, however, I started receiving calls, first from some heads of Italian banks and then from associations representing consumers. They wanted to know what the Italian government intended to do about the many Italian investors who had bought Argentine bonds. This would have been a strange question in the United States, but not in Italy where the government is seen as the cause of most problems and the promoter of most solutions.

Progressively, I discovered that: (a) the Italians who had bought the bonds were not a few but almost half million; (b) they had bought about $15 billion of Argentine bonds or about 1 percent of Italy's GDP; and (c) most of them were not the sophisticated investors that I had originally expected, but people of modest means and limited education who, in some cases, had put their lifetime savings in this presumably higher return asset, after the interest rates on Italian bonds had fallen as a result of Italy joining the European Monetary Union. Many Italians would suffer (obviously on a smaller scale) the same consequences as their counterparts in the Argentine middle class: they would lose a significant part of their wealth. I started receiving visits from some of these investors. On one occasion, an elderly couple well into their eighties, poorly dressed and obviously not highly educated, came to my office and cried in my presence explaining that their lifetime savings had been invested in Argentine bonds. They would be ruined and left without any means for the rest of their lives. They had been told by their financial adviser that this was a good and safe investment. Obviously, there was not much that the Italian government could do about it and many Italians could not believe that Argentina, the rich country to which many

Italians had emigrated for a century, did not have enough assets to pay them in other ways. Some asked why Argentina could not pay them with land.

The more I thought about this situation, the more upset I became with the IMF. I recalled the many misgivings I had had over several years about the Fund's relationship with Argentina and the reports I had sent to the Fund management. I asked myself what responsibility the IMF might have toward these individuals. When the IMF enters in a lending program with a country that is borrowing not only from the Fund and from the sophisticated and well-informed Wall Street investment bankers, *but also from badly-informed and inexperienced individuals*, such as the old, uneducated couple that came to my office, what's the extent of the IMF's responsibility to send *clear and totally honest signals* about the chances of success in the country and the risks that individuals would run in investing in the bonds issued by that country? The Fund failed to realize that the ongoing financial globalization was changing the nature of the game. More and more, the global financial market included actions by small, unsophisticated investors in addition to those of the "fat cats" from Wall Street. With the passing of time, the financial market was assuming some of the characteristics of the eBay market, which is accessible to everyone. I felt that the signals sent by the Fund over the years had not always been clear or completely honest. Occasionally, they had been much too optimistic. I kept thinking of Michel Camdessus' statement about Argentina at the 1998 Annual Meetings. But this had not been the only example of rosy statements. The public information notices (PINs) that came out of the discussions by the Executive Board of the IMF about other countries had often had the same ring. They tended to put the nicest face possible to situations that were often far worse than reported. Optimism was a way of attracting foreign investors. And, as long as money kept rolling in, a country's situation was considered viable.

Small investors do not have an independent way of assessing risks and spreading them over many investments. Many may not even fully understand that higher returns on an asset often mean higher risks. Inevitably, these small investors get their signals from those who sell them the bonds (whose incentives are to sell the bonds and who, themselves, may be misled about the real risks) and occasionally from media statements that are in turn based on information that comes out of the IMF. The democratization or the "eBayzation" of the international financial market, in which many small investors participate, should have some implication on how the Fund conducts its business. It requires a higher degree of clarity and honesty by the IMF than in the past. At times, when I heard a public statement from Fund spokesmen that things were going well for a country, I thought, and occasionally I had information to prove it, that this was not the case. When the IMF enters in a lending program with a country that is borrowing not only from the Fund and from investment banks, but also from common people, it has the responsibility to send the clearest signals that convey *precisely and honestly* the dangers and the risks. These signals would reduce the chance that individuals risk their lifelong savings in what amounts to a gambling activity.

In early 2004, I sent a letter to the *Financial Times* in reaction to an editorial that argued that those who had bought Argentine bonds should have known what they were doing and, thus, should accept a large reduction in their repayment (a large "haircut" in the jargon), while the debt owed to the international financial institutions, and especially to the IMF, should be repaid in full. I asked whether it would be fair for Argentina to pay 100 percent of what it owed to the Fund but only a small proportion (around 30 percent) of what it owed to the Italian savers, as the Argentine government was proposing at that time. This letter questioned the special status of IMF loans. IMF loans had not been affected by the default and were expected to be paid in full. Obviously, this letter was not welcomed by the IMF. After it was published, Guillermo Calvo, then the chief economist at the IDB, where I was working as a consultant after my return from Italy, sent me an e-mail saying that after the publication of the letter my portrait had been put up, next to that of Joe Stiglitz, in the Fund's shooting gallery. Of course he was joking. Stiglitz was obviously not loved in the Fund because of his sharp and, at times, unfair criticism of Fund employees and Fund policies.

At the time of the renegotiations between Argentina and the non-official creditors, Argentina managed to dramatically reduce its large foreign debt through a "haircut" that cut the size of the debt and replaced expensive debt with cheap debt. The representative of the Italian bond holders declined to accept Argentina's offer so that, by the summer of 2007, Italian bondholders have still not been repaid any of their loans. The Italian government was considering the use of balances in some long-dormant bank accounts to make some restitution to small bondholders. Thus, after all, the Italian government may become a contributor to the solution to the defaulted assets for small shareholders.

I have not been involved with developments in Argentina since the default. I visited Argentina briefly in 2004 to attend a tax conference organized by the InterAmerican Development Bank and stayed in Buenos Aires only a short time. At that time, the main news was that of the "piqueteros," individuals who were occupying McDonalds and asking for large contributions to the poor. Questions related to the protection of property rights were being asked and the government was being criticized for not being more forceful in defending them.

I am glad to report that after 2002, when the Argentine GDP fell by 10.9 percent, after the sharp falls in 2000 and 2001, and unemployment reached 21 percent, the country started growing at substantial rates (8.7 percent in 2003, 9.0 percent in 2004, 9.2 percent in 2005, and 8.5 percent in 2006). A large part of the growth after 2002 has been due to a recovery from the loss in output experienced in 2000–2002. In 2006, the *per capita* GDP recovered the 1998 level, while *total* GDP was 12 percent higher than in 1998. In 2005, 34 percent of the population was still in poverty, down from the 57 percent in 2002. Unemployment fell from 21 percent in 2002 to about 10 percent in 2006. This is better than it was in the 1990s.

The elimination of a large portion of the most costly foreign debt helped Argentina improve its fiscal situation, because of the large saving that it generated on interest payments. It needed a much lower primary surplus to service the debt. The large devaluation, at the beginning of a commodity boom, helped its exports. The pesoification of domestic debt sharply reduced the debt of the enterprises. However, because of the large devaluation of its currency, the share of the foreign debt into GDP remains large. Its cost is much lower because of the elimination of the high interest debt and its replacement with much cheaper debt. The servicing of the public debt continues to be a significant claim on fiscal revenue and still requires significant primary surpluses. The country risk has been rising and, in June 2007, it reached 300 basis points. The fiscal accounts have improved because the government succeeded, for a while, in keeping public expenditure under control and especially in raising the tax level. Real wages for public employees continue to be well below the period before the default in spite of some recent catching-up. Roberto Lavagna, the economy minister for much of this period, negotiated with creditors the arrangements that followed the default. He got a very good deal for Argentina, but some claims by foreign investors remain unsettled.

Some of the expenditure cuts, especially in real wages and in investment, are not likely to be sustainable over the longer run and some of them will negatively affect the economy in the future. Lavagna resigned in November 2005, in part because wages had been allowed to start growing at a faster pace than he thought desirable. Total public spending (including the national public sector and the provinces) has started increasing again, having risen by about 2 percent of GDP between 2004 and 2006 in spite of the fast growth of GDP. The tax burden was pushed to the record level of about 27 percent of GDP in 2006, or about 6 percent of GDP *above* previous records. Much of the increase in taxes has come from a tax on financial transactions and from "temporary" taxes on exports. The commodity boom and the large devaluation have made these taxes possible, and perhaps even justifiable on equity grounds, for the time being. It should be recalled that export taxes played a significant role during the first Perón era, when they generated large revenue to finance the growing public spending. Both of these taxes are extraordinarily distortive. They ought to be eliminated as soon as possible before they do major damage to the economy. However, the revenue that these taxes generate has accounted for all primary surplus that Argentina had in 2005 and 2006.

Thus, Argentina is back to the situation I described in the second chapter, when a *temporary* fiscal equilibrium is achieved by an *exceptional* tax effort and/or by *unsustainable* cuts in public spending. At this time, the fiscal equilibrium is being helped by the exceptionally good international situation and by the still undervalued exchange rate. Exceptional tax efforts and unsustainable cuts in public spending, by definition, cannot be maintained, over the long run. I would be surprised and pleased if the current fiscal situation were maintained, but I fear that this will be difficult. There are already worrisome signs. In spite of the increase in the share of total taxes into GDP in 2004–2006 (by almost 2 percent of GDP), total consolidated, primary surplus has fallen by an equivalent amount fully reflecting a deterioration in the accounts of the provincial governments. The fiscal behavior of these government is likely to play, again, a major role in the future.

As it happened with previous governments, sooner or later the current administration will face the problem of unsustainable fiscal outcomes generated by a *role of the state* in the economy; that in a substantive way, has not changed. This role will continue to require more public spending than the country will be able to finance through ordinary revenue. Without the anchor of the Convertibility Law, that might mean a return to pressures on the Central Bank, and to inflationary finance, especially because foreign borrowing will be more difficult. Inflation has been raising its head and it reached 12.3 percent in 2005. It fell a little in 2006 as a result of price controls and possible manipulation of the price index. There has been a return to some administrative controls of prices and wages. This has happened in the area of the tariffs of public utilities—which may contribute to problems in the energy sector, because the low prices have discouraged new investment in energy sources, and in the prices of beef and milk. I hope I am wrong, but my understanding of the fiscal history of Argentina over the past sixty years does not make me optimistic about the future in spite of the good performance of the economy in the 2003–2007 period.

Sooner or later, the fiscal cycles are likely to reestablish themselves. Then, Argentina will have to deal with a still-large public debt, owed partly to international financial institutions and to creditors who already got a substantial "haircut." An eventual debt rescheduling would be far more difficult than the last one. But, if it ever happened, that would be in the distant future. For the time being, this is another good period for Argentina. The sun has been shining again over Buenos Aires and God seems to have reclaimed, at least for the time being, his Argentine citizenship.

In 2006, the government repaid in full its debt to the IMF, borrowing dollars that the Central Bank had accumulated as a consequence of the large trade surplus that Argentina had been running in recent years. The books of the Central Bank now have government bonds instead of dollar reserves; thus, in some sense the quality of the Central Bank's assets has fallen. The payment of the debt owed to the IMF means that the country's relation with the Fund will not tie the hands of Néstor Kirchner, the current president, or of future governments. The IMF should have been happy with this repayment but, in an ironical twist of faith, it has discovered that the repayment by Argentina, Brazil, and other former large debtors, has created income problems for the Fund, forcing it to introduce, internally, austerity measures of the kind that it unsuccessfully tried to introduce in Argentina. For the time being, there are no dark clouds for Argentina . As for a more distant future, who knows? As the song goes: "Que será, será."

Index of Names